ON TRIAL

Lessons from a Lifetime in the Courtroom

Henry G. Miller, Esq.

ALM Publishing
New York

Cover Design: *Michael Ng*
Interior Page Design & Production: *Amparo Graf*

Library of Congress Cataloging-in-Publication Data

Miller, Henry G., 1931-
    On trial : lessons from a lifetime in the courtroom / Henry G. Miller.
      p. cm.
    ISBN 0-9705970-4-5
    1. Trial practice—United States.

KF8915 .M475 2001
347.73'75—dc21
                                             2001033654

"Henry Miller's *On Trial* is an instructive collection of common sense lessons drawn from the author's vast courtroom experience. Lawyers will appreciate the author's breezy, natural style, savoring his pithy insights and wickedly astute observations. This feast of wit and wisdom is both useful and fun to read by lawyers and anyone else."

Joseph W. Bellacosa,
Dean, St. John's Law School,
former New York State Court of Appeals Judge

"*On Trial* is a must read for both new lawyers and seasoned trial attorneys. Henry Miller, an experienced, well regarded advocate, manages to capture the essence of his experiences over four decades in the courtroom. In a most readable fashion he provides insightful information concerning all elements of a trial from picking a jury to summation. The Prologue, entitled 'Trying Your First Case? Nineteen Tiny Tips,' should be required reading for all lawyers who are about to try their first case. The chapter on 'Living with Defeat' provides good advice to even experienced trial lawyers about how to put defeat in perspective and overcome a trial loss. In addition to providing a concise trial advocacy primer for busy practitioners, this book's wisdom comes with a touch of humor."

Sheila L. Birnbaum,
Skadden, Arps, Slate, Meagher & Flom LLP

"As one who has tried cases for almost four decades, *On Trial* is a 'must read,' full of nuggets of wit and wisdom, a veritable panoply of prescriptions for success for the modern day trial lawyer."

Johnnie L. Cochran, Jr.

"There's no substitute for experience, and this fine book teaches some excellent lessons from the school of hard knocks. Read it and learn."

Alan M. Dershowitz,
Author of Supreme Injustice

"Every trial lawyer can learn a lot from this book, written by one of the great trial lawyers of our time. These valuable, down to earth, common sense tips cover everything from jury selection to summation in an entertaining and highly readable style."

Robert B. Fiske, Jr.,
Davis Polk and Wardwell, formerly United States Attorney
for the Southern District of New York

"Superb! You will read this again and again—first as a masterly text of trial tactics, and then as a philosophy of life as seen through the eyes of a trial lawyer. Henry Miller is a nonpareil."

Harvey Weitz,
Trial Lawyer and Author

Dedication

To the Gagliardis: Frank, Joe and Lee,
to whom I owe much.

Acknowledgments

I have borrowed, cited, quoted and stolen so much from other trial lawyers that I'm reminded of the old quip: plagiarism among lawyers is called research.

I started to list all those whose ideas, strategies, routines and clever remarks I've shamelessly purloined over the years. But the list grew so long that it threatened to become a separate book which nobody except those listed would read. Also, there was the fear of leaving out some worthy who might take revenge on me. I was beginning to sound like those breathless types who upon receiving an Academy Award start by thanking their kindergarten teacher and conclude with their funeral director to-be.

Therefore, I decided to just list a few of those who have already gone to their reward. So if you're not on the list, be happy, it probably means you're still alive.

Matthew Lawless—my first mentor. From him I learned, integrity is all.

Jack Bachkoff, Irv Segal, Alex Rosenthal, Morris Zweibel, Milt Steger and Mort Jacobs—my next mentors, from whom I learned you have to be brave when the jury hates you, you have to put it all in perspective when you lose and you have to know the law even if you're only a trial lawyer.

John Reilly, Harry Gair, Emile Zola Berman, Jack Fuchsberg, Al Julien and Mike Hayes, the luminaries of the trial bar when I began, from whom I learned the excitement of legal combat.

The Westchester lawyers, Denny O'Connor, Don Mead, Jim Dempsey, Grenny Keogh, Big Don Wilson, Little Don Wilson, Billy Bave, Joe Buderwitz, Frank Henderson, Joe Woods, Henry Smith, Frank Young and Dick Daronco, from whom I learned friendship is advocacy's reward.

Introduction

WHY?

Another book for trial lawyers? Aren't we already drowning in a flood of never-ending how-to texts? There are tomes upon tomes sketching in detail the trial lawyer's every travail and trauma. Manuals on advocacy, supplemented yearly, encyclopedic in scope, saturate every law library. But that's the problem.

No one, and certainly not busy practitioners, can read more than a mere fraction of the available literature.

But there's a problem with such a mountain of erudition. Few bother to climb it. They don't have the time. Life is short. Who can deal with all this information spun out by young researchers and tireless computers? In this, the "Age of More Information Than We Know What to Do With," we need brevity.

When we read great literature, we should not rush. We should dally, savor and enjoy. But that's for Dickens and Tolstoy. When it comes to the technical texts of our trade, we need speed. There may be gold in those mountainous volumes, but we want it mined for us. Busy trial lawyers nowadays don't have the luxury of reading all the available wonderful texts on the art of advocacy.

The books of the past that have become classics prove the point. Lloyd Paul Stryker's Art of Advocacy has been reprinted many times. His articles were not encyclopedic. They were not updated yearly. Rather, they were a distillation of what he learned from a lifetime in the courtroom.

THIS BOOK

Some years ago, I was asked by the New York Law Journal to become a columnist on the subject of "Trials." This was an opportunity that I gladly accepted. I decided to write on each phase of the trial. Intending no presumption, the articles were well received. One judge who taught a course on trial advocacy used them in his teaching. Many asked me over the years to make a book of them.

And so I have. I don't claim to be one of the foremost authorities on how to try a case. Many trial lawyers have better credentials and have had more celebrated cases. But, after more than four decades of actively trying cases, participating in many seminars and exchanging with my colleagues what hopefully passes for a little wisdom, I'd be dull indeed not to have drawn a few conclusions.

I wrote these articles, always striving for brevity, for the young lawyer embarking on a career in the courtroom. I also wrote them for those at the peak of their prowess. Hopefully, there is something for them as well. And I also wrote for my fellow seasoned seniors whose lives have been spent confronting demanding jurists, disagreeable witnesses, difficult jurors and dour clients. Perhaps my words will now and then bring a smile of recognition to their faces. That would please me most of all and be my most satisfying reward.

Contents

TRYING YOUR FIRST CASE?
NINETEEN
TINY TIPS

J EREMIAH SAGE, THE BARD OF THE BROOKLYN BAR, LOVED nothing more than talking to young lawyers. He found in them the enthusiasm which had all too often leaked away from many of his aging peers. Lawyers about to try their first case often visited his office high above the crowds on Court Street. Legendary were his "tiny tips," some of which are excerpted here.

1.   *Forget Yourself.* You're nervous. Of course. It's your first trial. The secret: forget yourself.

Some years ago, Nick Noviss was sent to court to answer the calendar. He had never tried a case. The calendar judge, Nigel Noheart, known as No Excuse Nigel, a marvel of unreasonableness, thundered, "Mr. Noviss, pick the jury. You're admitted to the Bar, aren't you? Not another word. Take the jury slip." Noviss took the jury slip and promptly fainted. That's a bad start. What was he doing wrong? He was thinking of himself. "How do I look?" "Am I dressed right?" Forget yourself. You're not important. Think of the case. The case is important.

2. *Love Your Nerves.* The jury will see it. They'll love you because you're nervous. Maybe they'll even protect you.

3. *Tell Them It's Your First Case.* "I'm sorry, Mr. Foreman, I didn't mean to hand you the document. It's my first trial." "Oh, forgive me, Judge, I forgot to stand. It's my first trial." It's a hard-hearted jury who will hurt you in your first trial. With a little ingenuity, you can use this line a few times. "Oh, it's my first criminal case." "My first arbitration." "My first case in Brooklyn."

However, it's considered bad form and against our union rules to use the line more than five times.

4. *Love Your Client.* You're no longer at a trial seminar in law school. You now represent a flesh and blood client. Know that client. Identify with that client. Care for your client. Say for her what she cannot say for herself. Is that not the very origin of our profession? Your concern and passion will shine through everything you do.

5. *Just Say "Objection."* Among the greatest mysteries facing the new lawyer is what, if anything, that massive body of rules, precedents, confusions and ambiguities known as the rules of evidence has to do with the conduct of a trial.

Mr. Slick, a senior and cagy litigator, offers a collection of newspaper articles describing the case at hand. You sit there alone. You have no adviser. You know it doesn't sound right. You were there the day in law school they talked about hearsay. The professor said something about "unreliable." But how to keep it out? You've heard a memo of law helps but you didn't expect this offer and you don't have one. You've heard a motion in advance of trial can sometimes keep out unsavory material. But it's too late for that. The jury is looking at you. The judge is looking at you. What to do? How do you keep "it" out?

Now hear this and learn the first rule of evidence: just stand and say, "Objection." The judge may amaze you and say, "Sustained."

You'll be timid at first, but after a while you might grow to love it. Some lawyers have become so obsessed with their right, their duty, to object, that they cannot live without their objections. This is particularly true of craggy old defense lawyers. Some are so addicted to their objections that they rarely find any evidence they consider admissible.

6.   *Ask Questions.* Annoy your friends. Badger your superiors. "What should I ask the police officer?" "How much should I say in the fact portion of my trial brief?" "Does this judge have any pet peeves?" "Should I object to their economist?" "How do you cross-examine a pathologist?" There are no dumb questions. Well, almost none. There are, however, dumb lawyers. Who are they? Lawyers who don't ask questions.

Incidentally, when you're ninety-three and about to start your four hundredth trial, you should still be asking questions. How do you know when it's time to stop trying cases? When you stop asking questions.

7.   *Don't Shoot Every Mosquito.* Samuel Sly loves to bait young lawyers. He distracts them with minor points. "The contract was signed at 3 P.M., not 2 P.M." Mr. Nu, trying his first case, wastes precious energy and time proving it was 2 P.M. The judge has already ruled it doesn't matter what time it was signed. The issue is whether there was fraud in the inducement. Don't take the bait. Don't use cannons to shoot mosquitoes.

8.   *Make Lists.* Mr. Big Memree boasts: I never forget. I don't make lists. They would interfere with my creativity. But, in his last trial, he forgot to read the key part of the deposition which established who owned the factory building. Defense counsel moved to dismiss because there was no proof of ownership. Big Memree had to beg Judge Kindly to let him reopen. Kindly said: "Alright, but in the future, make a list." Indeed. List the points you have to prove. List the exhibits you want to introduce. List the witnesses you want to call. Why burden your memory?

9. *Overprepare.* This is the beginner's advantage. Know every word. Know every fact. Preparation alleviates anxiety. With advancing age and many trials behind you, it gets harder to read the file in all its tedious detail. You have to fight the ennui of marking up the depositions. You have done it over and over.

But when it's your first case, it's springtime in Paris. Everything is possible. Life is unfolding before you. There has never been such a case. To the seasoned veteran, it may only be a minuscule misdemeanor, but to you it is alive with constitutional implications. To the aging advocate, it may be just another intersection accident, but to you it is nothing less than a dispute over human rights.

You have beginner's zeal. Therefore, read everything twice. Personally interview every potential witness. Have your opening and your questioning of witnesses blocked out before you even pick the first juror.

You can even strike terror into your veteran opponent's heart. You are the most dangerous of all adversaries: A first-time trial lawyer oblivious of the fact that you're supposed to lose the case.

10. *Watch Other Trials.* You can learn from the best, particularly from their mistakes. Besides, it's the entertainment of real life. And it's free. Most television shows and movies are operating at a fifth-grade level. So watch trials instead. And if you hear of a great trial from the past, read the transcript. It's faster than watching a trial and you can learn much. You will already know who won or lost.

11. *Be Yourself.* This is the most difficult of the tips. It takes years to be yourself. Willa Cather spoke to writers but could have been speaking to us: "Only the practiced hand can make the natural gesture." But you must try. Talk as if in conversation. Don't make speeches. Use plain words. Say "car," not "vehicle." Don't use lawyer's jargon. Say "jury selection," not "voir dire."

Explain the case to your spouse, your secretary, or even better, some bright cynical teenagers. They will not tolerate artificiality. They will expect genuineness.

By all means, go to seminars and learn from the "masters." But remember the masters have their own clay feet and their style may not ring true in your mouth. By imitating no one and just trying to be natural, the day may come when you will be as relaxed in the courtroom as in your living room. And then you will ring true.

12. *Be Innovative.* Never do anything *pro forma*. Think of a new and better way. Think. Think. You might even be able to show the know-it-all old-timers a thing or two.

13. *Be Respectful.* Sure, you've heard how tough trial lawyers stand up to hostile judges. So you're not going to back down. Be careful. Ms. Chipon Shoulder has waited too long for her chance to show the world she's fearless. She disagrees with the judge every chance she gets. She fights over every ruling and she's quite pleased with herself. P.S. The jury hates her.

Ms. Charmen Smile is strong but deferential. She seeks to make the judge an ally. "May I call a witness now?" "Am I allowed to speak on that point, Your Honor?" P.S. The jury loves her.

Most jurors trust judges and look for cues as to their leanings. Fighting with the Court is an acquired skill reserved for those curmudgeonly veterans who would dry up and die without the exquisite joy of baiting judges.

14. *Be Up Front.* Any problems in your case? Talk about them in jury selection and opening. Don't be slick and hide. Any bad documents that you know are admissible? You'd better offer them. Be up front. Win the jurors' trust. They're looking to see if you are trustworthy. They want integrity. This approach will serve you well all your career.

15. *Be Confident.* Don't look like a whipped dog. Jurors want to know you believe in your case. They may not understand all the technical evidence but they know the human face. They search your face for clues. But at all costs, you must:

16. *Never Be Arrogant.* Jurors hate it. Arrogance is unacceptable in even the most celebrated and successful of advocates. In a beginner, it is absurd and laughable. So if you're one of those spoiled and strutting newcomers who think the world is waiting for you, let me assure you, it's not. Every thought and ambition you have, your elders have already had.

If you have a problem in this area, read Jonathan Swift—at least the last few pages of *Gulliver's Travels.* Know your place. Don't take yourself too seriously. Think about the human condition five minutes a day. That will cure you of arrogance.

17. *Don't Settle.* (Sage is particularly worth quoting here.)

> *"How will you ever be a trial lawyer if you settle every case? When I was young, I'd cry if the case was settled. Now I cry if it isn't. But I've had thousands of trial days and already proven I have the fortitude to take verdicts. If this is your first case and you're desperate to settle it, find another line of work."*

But what if your client's interests are best served by a settlement? Why then you must settle. But just make sure that in your heart you're ready to take a verdict. Incidentally, that's the best way to settle a case.

18. *Keep Quiet.* Learn when to shut up. Young lawyers invariably talk too much. Never say one word more than is necessary.

Talk less and sit more. Silence shows strength. Knowing when not to talk is another acquired skill. Learn it early.

19. *Be Kind.* Just remember as you try to demolish your aging opponent that the day will come when some youngster will come swaggering down the aisle anxious to take the title away from you.

Chapter 1

THE FORTY-FOUR
MOST COMMON BLUNDERS OF
JURY SELECTION

"The efficiency of our jury . . . system is only marred by the difficulty of finding twelve men every day who don't know anything and can't read."

— Mark Twain

T RUDGING BACK FROM COURT, AFTER DEFEAT IN A JURY TRIAL, wildly in search of some explanation other than my own inadequacy, I have often thought of the old saw, "the case was decided thirty years ago." Yes, that's it: not even the devil or Daniel Webster could have rooted out the prejudice of "that jury." But, wait a minute. My victorious opponent also selected that jury. Was the enemy wiser than I? More astute in challenging? More able to indoctrinate? Is there an art to selecting a jury? Educated by that most masterful of human teachers, DEFEAT, let us try to identify the most common and egregious blunders of jury selection in those jurisdictions where the lawyers conduct the voir dire themselves.

1.   *Insulting the Jury.* Mr. Barrister makes his magnificent statement to the jury. He then loftily inquires of Mr. Meek, juror number one, "Do you understand?" The implication, of course, is that any failure of understanding is of necessity due to the limited mental capacity of the juror. Mr. Meek is insulted. Mr. Barrister is insulting. A mere touch of humility would have corrected the question to, "Have I made myself clear?"

Other outstanding advocates of our generation will inquire of some fifty-year-old gentleman, "How long have you been a messenger?" It might be preferable to ask the juror about the nature of his work so that he can protect himself in the language he chooses. We never know exactly when a juror makes his or her decision. But it would appear questionable to start by insulting the juror.

2. *Talking Too Much.* Mr. Advocate pours forth words in a greater flood than Niagara Falls. Mr. Cynical, juror number two, is intensely suspicious. He sees the lawyer as a salesman. Why say one word more than necessary? It has been suggested that no lawyer should ever say one word in any trial without a reason. It can make us more interesting. The jurors will begin to await our statements.

3. *Succumbing to the Itch to Be Brilliant.* Mr. Luminous of the office of Vanity, Fair and Pride loves big words, adores legal jargon and asks complicated questions. Mr. Carpenter on the jury thinks this lawyer is a show-off. He thinks the lawyer is trying to trick him. He thinks if the lawyer had a good case, he would talk simply and fairly. Yes, humility is the trial lawyer's best friend.

4. *Failure to Follow the Principle of Identification.* Simply stated, it means we should seek jurors who identify with us and our clients. We should reject jurors who identify with our adversaries. When the occupation of Juror Jones is the same as that of our Client Smith, it is to our advantage. If the juror lives in the same area where our client lives, it is another advantage. We even like jurors who have the same first name as we do. Anything which tends to make them identify with us is, in the ordinary course of human events, helpful to our side. There are exceptions to every guiding principle, but here is a starting point that will ring true more often than not. One remembers hearing of a famous criminal trial involving celebrated defendants. Psychological studies were supposedly employed to help identify the ideal jurors who would help these defendants. The jury was selected along the lines suggested by the studies. When challenges were exhausted, an alternate juror was selected who did not fit the pattern established by the psychological study. This juror was a successful man—an executive. The study had suggested that people of a lower economic status would be more favorable to the defendants, who were very successful men of national standing. During the trial, the alternate came to sit on the jury in chief. He dominated deliberations. He favored the defendants. There was a defendants' verdict. The psychological study was wrong. The principle of identification proved its value.

5. *Failure to Challenge the Array.* The panel walks in. You once read that it's impossible to judge a book by its cover, but you are crushed by what you see. You are defending a client accused of assaulting a little old lady, and everybody on this jury looks like a police officer. Listen carefully. Your opponent may be carried away. Note every word that may have prejudice in it. Accumulate them, and remember the ancient Ciceronian rule of jury selection: when all is lost, challenge the array.

6. *Failure to Assert a Challenge for Cause.* In ancient days, the English crown had unlimited peremptory challenges. You do not. You cannot afford to be lazy. If Mr. Equivocal, a prospective juror whom you despise, is on the fence, at least appeal to his fairness. "Sir, considering that the parties have waited some years for their day in court for a completely impartial jury, you will of course tell us, will you not, if you have any doubt at all—won't you? Please! Please?" When that fails, you will, of course, use a peremptory challenge.

7. *Stupidly Using Your Last Challenge.* You have one challenge remaining. You are reasonably satisfied with all the jurors, but you have a mild doubt about Mrs. Bland. You use your last challenge. You are suing an automobile manufacturer. On comes Mr. Big, president of a manufacturing company. He insists he will be fair. The Judge, whom you see quietly in chambers, tells you that you do not have a challenge for cause. Oh, Death, where is thy sting?

8. *Stupidly Not Using Your Last Challenge.* The jury is satisfactory, except for one person. You represent a teacher who claims she was wrongfully dismissed. On the jury is Mr. Dean, a principal of a school who has had vicious disputes with many teachers over the question of tenure. He has been glaring at you and your client during jury selection. You have one challenge remaining. However, you once went to a seminar where somebody said, "Don't use your last challenge." You do not use your last challenge. That juror kills you. You lose the case. You took the advice too literally.

9. *Keeping the Expert Juror or the Take-Charge Juror.* You have the burden of proving a chemical reaction occurred. Mr. Chemist has four degrees in the field. He will, of course, have to demonstrate his erudition by showing how you failed to prove the chemical reaction. He will awe the other jurors. RULE: *Take no expert unless you are positive your evidence must prevail.* This is also true for Ms. Ringleader. If you believe you have a fair cause, you really don't need the assistance of Mr. Domineering. Maybe the art of jury selection is avoiding the strong juror who will oppose you.

10. *Sleeping During Jury Selection.* There are many ways to sleep during jury selection. Some do it by constantly taking notes. Some by talking to other lawyers during recess. Better to observe the juror when he takes his seat. Mr. Military walks briskly. Mr. Clerk, hesitantly. We learn much by the way jurors dress, the faces they make and at whom they smile. Some say you never know what a jury will do; we reply: it is our job to know what a jury will do. A grand time to watch jurors is when your opponent is speaking. Is Ms. Susceptible in love with my opponent, Mr. Tall, Dark and Handsome? Challenge! Challenge!

11. *Not Establishing Your Credibility.* Mr. Weasel, a lawyer, says something to one juror but tries to change it when he speaks to another juror. He has weaseled. His credibility may be irrevocably lost. You, the trial lawyer, are the chief witness for your cause. You will say more on behalf of your client than any witness. If "character" is the chief quality of the advocate, not one word must ever be devious.

12. *Not Sounding the Theme.* Mr. Pointless talked at length but the jurors don't recall what he said. He never made a point. As in music there is a grand line, so in every lawsuit there is a theme. You are defending a medical doctor charged with malpractice. Your defense is that your client used her best judgment. You have but three opportunities to address a jury directly in a trial: jury selection, opening and summation. It is an irretrievable loss of one of your opportunities not to sound the theme of "judgment" no matter how subtly during voir dire. Repetition is a valid tool of persuasion. *Make your point.*

13. *Overstating the Case.* Mr. Blunder represents Ms. Devastated, who has lost an eye and a leg. She was standing on a sidewalk when Mr. Drunk, the intoxicated defendant, drove his car onto the sidewalk. Mr. Blunder pours it on. He pounds the jurors with all the facts. Defendant's attorney, Mr. Crafty, merely says: "Will you keep an open mind?" Jurors must say yes and they say yes. The "oomph" is gone. Many jurors outraged at defendant's drinking have excused themselves. All Mr. Blunder had to say is: "We claim a significant injury due to defendant's negligence." Let Mr. Crafty, defendant's attorney, sit on the horns of the dilemma. If Crafty says nothing in jury selection, plaintiff's opening will be an atomic explosion. If Crafty admits the serious injury and the drink, (1) he will have to struggle awkwardly with his words, (2) plaintiff's attorney's understatement will enhance plaintiff's attorney's credibility, and (3) the jury will surely believe it if Crafty has to admit it.

14. *Disclosing Significant Weaknesses.* Mr. Innocent, your client, has a criminal record. Nothing is said about that in jury selection. On cross-examination, your opponent, Mr. Relentless, pursues your client devastatingly with his criminal record. The jury is shocked. You see your cause and fee flowing down the drain. Why didn't you say during jury selection: "My client, I want you to know, committed some indiscretions at a young age (it's always at a young age) for which he paid the penalty exacted by the law. He now has a case that is in no way related to his past. Can you give him a fair trial?"

15. *Not Objecting to "Just Because."* Mr. Ploy likes to do more than disclose and defuse the weaknesses in his case. He likes to literally obliterate them. He usually starts with "just because." "Just because my client, who had five martinis on an empty stomach, and went through the red light when he was in a drag race at eighty miles an hour before he hit the child on the sidewalk, that is not something you would hold against him, is it?" Please wake up, my friend, and object. It is indeed the jury's role to hold some sins against some people.

16. *Failure to Embrace the Law.* Bill Blunder, plaintiff's attorney, says nothing about the law. Ms. Moses, defendant's attorney, embraces the law as if she were on Mt. Sinai. The jury clearly understands that the law favors the defendant. **MORAL:** *Embrace the law, whether you love it or not.* If you don't, your opponent will. Of course, if there are aspects of the law that are, shall we say, at odds with your view of the case, you can speak more softly and with less gusto.

17. *Not Practicing the Art of "What's Left in the Back Anyway?"* You've been selecting a jury for three hours. The jury is reasonable. You have a doubt. You excuse two jurors. In walk Mr. Awful and Mr. Worse. You die. You hadn't studied what was left. **MORAL:** *Try to know what's left.* If their names were called out when they entered, jot them down. Study them as they walk, talk, act and respond. How are they dressed? Watch them while you're selecting the jurors-in-chief. Have you noticed whether those left think your opponent is a humorous fellow or an annoying show-off? It is idle indeed to keep searching for the Holy Grail of the unattainable perfect jury when what is in the box is better than what is left. This requires the use of judgment. Jury selection in truth is really jury rejection.

18. *Not Confronting the Ugly Juror.* Mr. Misanthrope, a member of the jury panel, is glaring at everybody. He has announced that the lawyers don't know what they are doing nor are they fair. He does not understand why we have to have lawsuits. He doesn't understand why we need juries. The other jurors look at him uneasily. Ms. Polyanna, plaintiff's lawyer, tries to placate him. Why bother? While normally we avoid offense to any prospective juror, there are times for us to assert candidly our displeasure. We have every right to tell him that the parties to this lawsuit have waited for years for a jury to resolve the dispute. Jury trials are the alternative to the use of force. Without further ado, you can tell him his attitude is not acceptable and that you excuse him. While you perhaps have been more harsh than usual, what has happened? You have enhanced your credibility. Trial lawyers need not be obsequious.

19. *Failing to Unmask the Sneaky Challenger.* Mr. Sneaky slips the slip to the clerk. The juror is excused. No one knows by whom. The antidote: in your loudest trial lawyer's voice, ask the clerk, "Whose challenge was that?" This ploy and counterploy have been going on since Demosthenes wowed the Assembly in Old Athens.

20. *Not Letting the Juror Talk.* Mr. Big Mouth loves his voice. He asks only leading questions. The juror merely nods yes or no. Mr. Big Mouth wouldn't know whether he had Einstein or Frankenstein on the jury. MORAL: *Let the juror talk.* Ask "What do you think?" rather than "Do you think. . .?"

21. *Not Having a Plan.* Mr. Witless has no plan. He asks questions in a haphazard sequence. He has not thought out which jurors would be good or bad. Why give yourself that disadvantage? A few minutes with a colleague in the office talking over the jury selection will make you more confident when you arrive in

Court for jury selection. The main purpose of preparation has been to find your theme. Now you should plan to sound that theme. You should not disdain a checklist or a written order of sequence. You need not use it, but it will be there as a guide. We all have lapses of memory. An example of a possible sequence for an attorney who speaks first might be: (1) introduction of the parties and the attorneys; (2) whether the jurors know the parties or the attorneys; (3) the nature of the case; (4) whether the jurors know something of the witnesses or the issues of the case; (5) an exploration of the bias of the jurors; (6) whether there are any disqualifying facts; and (7) a conclusory statement. An example of a possible checklist of questions concerning bias and disqualification might include questions dealing with the following: (1) prior jury service; (2) the schooling and place of birth of the juror; (3) kinship, friendship, knowledge or financial interest as to any party, attorney, and maybe certain witnesses; (4) the marital status, including the number of children, of the juror; (5) the employment of the juror and the juror's family; (6) whether there was any prior experience with the kind of litigation which is presently before the court; and (7) a review of the juror's former and present residences. Obviously checklists are to be used selectively and without any stereotyped rigidity. Great advocacy can arise only through the use of imagination. However, imagination seems to function better when the advocate has a well-planned conception of the approach to be taken.

22. *Fighting with Your Opponent.* Mr. Pugnacious, along with some of our other friends at the Trial Bar, has perfected the art of enticing you into an unseemly dispute. He knows you have the better of the case. He wants a personality contest. **MORAL:** *A soft word turneth away wrath.* Keep your eye on the target. You have the better case. Be wary of dueling with an opponent known to have the fastest tongue in town.

23. *Not Fighting with Your Opponent.* Mr. Pugnacious has gone too far. He believes that a trial lawyer is one who appears on the surface to be a perfect gentleman, but underneath should have the corrupt heart of a riverboat gambler. He has this time thrown the gauntlet down and you cannot ignore it. Some snide remark about your position, which would rob you of any chance to win, has been made. You may feel that wit alone or a ruling by the Court is insufficient to deflect the remark. Then tell him off. You are not there merely to assert your position intellectually, but, if necessary, to protect your client by whatever honorable combat is required.

24. *Not Getting the Other Side to Challenge the Juror You Despise.* You are low on challenges. You hate juror number three. Walk up to him. Pretend that you love him, smile, get along beautifully, and hope that you confuse your opponent into challenging that juror.

25. *Canonizing the Juror You're About to Excuse.* You have made the firm decision to excuse juror two. For heaven's sake, don't keep asking her whether she can be fair and wonderful and decent in this case. She will, of course, say yes. When you excuse her, the other jurors will look at you curiously for letting St. Joan go.

26. *Failure to Use Voir Dire as an Instrument of Persuasion.* Mr. Laconic asks a few questions of each juror about their background. He then sits down. He never conveys any viewpoint about his case. Persuasion in jury selection is subtle and if overdone, it is clearly improper, but obviously we are always trying to influence. That is the role of the advocate and the jurors understand. Some lawyers believe that persuasion is the only purpose of jury selection. They say that human beings are so utterly unpredictable that the use of challenges is an empty gesture. You might just as well take the first six or twelve. While that philosophy is rejected by the bulk of trial lawyers, we are nevertheless reminded that the alternate purpose of jury selection—to convey our viewpoint—must never be ignored. For example, if you are a plaintiff in a personal injury case seeking a substantial award, you must ask the jurors whether they could make a substantial award. Many jurors have read critical reports in newspapers and magazines that verdicts are too high. You must explore whether each juror has an open mind:

> *"If after you hear **all** the evidence from the witnesses and the law from the court, you are convinced that the plaintiff should recover, would you be willing to vote for the plaintiff even if that evidence indicates in all fairness that there should be a substantial award?"*

You can then add quite properly that you regret talking about damages at this early point in the case. You know that they have not heard a word of evidence and may resent talk about money, but you can also quickly explain that this is the only opportunity you will have to explore the subject with them.

27. *Failure to Exploit the Juror Who Is Going to Go Anyway.* Your client sues for breach of express warranty made by a salesman. You wouldn't keep Mr. Salesman on the jury in any event. He's going to go. Why not use him to develop the proposition that even a salesman must respect the law that all products must fulfill the promises made of them. Then, at a later point, well after you have exploited him mercilessly, when all is forgotten, you will of course discreetly bounce him with an insensitivity that would have startled Caligula.

28. *Keeping Somebody You Don't Like.* On paper, Mrs. Perfect is perfect for you. She identifies in every way with your client. But you hate her. You don't know why. It gnaws at you. Excuse her. If you don't like her, she probably doesn't like you. GOLDEN RULE OF JURY SELECTION: *Pick not only with your brain but with your viscera.*

29. *Treating the Sexes Differently.* You approach the women on the jury. You ask each of them dutifully about her husband's occupation. You approach the men on the jury. You ask each of them about his occupation. You fail to ask each of them about his wife's occupation. Oh sin of sins! You have discriminated. Indeed you have. You treated the sexes differently. **MORAL:** *Be scrupulously alert to the nuances of gender.* Some female jurors do not wish to be called Miss or Mrs. but prefer Ms. The only problem is that other female jurors do not like the word "Ms." Good luck and you're on your own.

30. *Being Timid.* You represent the defendant. The plaintiff suffered grievous injuries from one of the defendant's employees who mugged her. The only issue is "scope of employment." Mr. Outraged looks at you when you ask whether he can be fair. He replies, "I don't know, there has been a lot of mugging in our area." You can meekly and timidly excuse the juror, which you may have to do in any event. However, this question is a great opportunity. You can state again your theme.

> *"There's no doubt, sir, that there has been much too much of this terrible crime of mugging. I can well understand why so many people are very, very upset. But the issue in this case is whether my client is liable for it. Will you give us a fair hearing?"*

You may not have defused the issue. You may never be able to defuse the issue. But you have at least addressed it without timidity.

31. *Not Keeping a Chart of the Jurors and a Record of Challenges.* Your opponent walks up to Mr. Hardnose. "Sir, thank you for your answers, but I'm going to challenge you." You look at your record. Good heavens! Your opponent has already used his last peremptory challenge. Your opponent turns blue; the Court denies his application for a challenge for cause. You turn to the juror and suggest, "You can be fair, sir, can you not?" You have kept a careful record of challenges; apparently your opponent did not. You need the names of the jurors on a chart with the other information concerning their residences, their occupations, and the special facts about them. You will want to review it during the trial as you prepare to make your various arguments to them. Only the careless lawyer does not have a chart or a record of the jurors.

32. *Continually Questioning the Juror You Love.* You've heard enough—you love Mrs. Sweetheart. But for some reason, you are mechanically wedded to your checklist. You represent a little child. You keep asking about all her children. Your opponent, Mr. Rip Van Winkle, who up to now has been satisfied, is aroused by one of the answers. He excuses her. **MORAL:** *When you have a juror you love, do not continue with your questions until you alert your opponent to the fact that you do love the juror.*

33. *Not Anticipating Your Opponent.* You represent a tragically maimed child who sues the manufacturer of pajamas for failure to make them flame retardant. Your opponent will obviously hammer away at the jury that they may not award damages merely because of sympathy. Therefore, you must steal your opponent's thunder. You must tell them in the first instance before your opponent speaks that you in no way want sympathy, which the lad has already abundantly received. Of course, plaintiff's attorney is always well-advised to keep his own ears open for defendant's plea for sympathy. Sometimes counsel for the defense will suggest that his corporate client really is "just a small business." Pleas for sympathy are inappropriate, no matter from whose mouth they come.

34. *Not Using the Motion in Limine.* Your client has been often arrested but never convicted. Evidence or questions as to the arrests are inadmissible. Your opponent, out of inexperience or for whatever reason, has indicated that be is going to develop that information during the voir dire. You have seen the panel of jurors arrive. It looks like it may be a very acceptable panel. You do not wish to risk anything prejudicial's being said to them. Your remedy is to apply to the Court and by a motion made in advance of the jury selection have your opponent restrained from using this inadmissible information.

35. *Engaging in Levity.* You represent the little child injured at the railroad crossing, where you claim there were inadequate guards. The injuries could make you cry. Your opponent, Mr. Jolly, is the prototype of the old railroad lawyer. Paternal, wise and experienced, he engages you and the jury in light banter. All of a sudden there is a light atmosphere. By the end of the case you don't know what's happening. You lose. You've been laughed out of Court. You wrongfully engaged in levity. Your cause was far too serious to permit that kind of mirth during jury selection.

36. *Not Engaging in Levity.* Your case is serious. You are appropriately serious. However, something natural to the proceedings, something inherent in the juror's own statement leads you to an expression with some wit. It relaxes everybody. You are further accepted as a human being. You have, without distracting from the enormity of your cause, handled the matter tactfully. You avoided the blunder of being a constant Mr. Sourpuss. In short, this is a tightrope that can be walked only by those who possess good judgment.

37. *Alienating the Jurors in a Strange Venue.* You are Mr. Celebrity. You are asked to journey to a different state to participate in a celebrated case. You get off the plane and are interviewed. You say that you strongly doubt whether you can get a fair jury in this jurisdiction. You walk into the jury room. Your attitude continues. You really don't expect the jury to be fair and it shows. The jury hates you and is rooting against you. You have poisoned the waters. When one thinks the venue is not capable of producing a fair trial, the remedy is not public insult but a discreet motion to the Court. If you lose your motion, you walk into the jury room and expect their fairness. It is elementary that we often receive from a person what we expect from a person. "I am not from your fine community. I believe that all people are entitled to a fair trial, not based on where a person's lawyer comes from." (And when toiling in foreign countries, never forget Aristotle's immortal advice: "Retain local counsel.")

38. *Ignoring Jurors' Attitudes.* You represent a patient who sues the local hospital and a local doctor because of claimed malpractice. There is no point in even trying that case unless counsel deals with the favored attitude benefiting those defendants. "We do not challenge the right of that hospital and that doctor to practice. We do not claim it is a bad hospital or he a bad doctor. We merely say that in this particular situation there was a departure from the required care, etc., etc."

39. *Searching for the Rules of Jury Selection.* There are no rules. There are only guides which supplement good judgment. Some are always in search of a talismanic device that will reduce jury selection to a rigid formula. It does not exist. Ignore articles that tell you in what case you need a juror who is an endomorph, or mesomorph, or an ectomorph or one who is brachycephalic (round-headed) or dolichocephalic (long-headed). You might as well study astrology and palm reading.

40. *Not Being Yourself.* Be yourself. But it's hard to be yourself. It takes experience. Willa Cather has said it is only the practiced hand that can make the natural gesture.

41. *Not Consulting with Your Client, Who Has Attended Jury Selection, Before Saying Satisfactory.* Let your client share in the compliment of saying "satisfactory." But don't consult with your client before challenging somebody.

42. *Mispronouncing the Juror's Name.* Miss Popo, she says clearly. You're not listening. You get up. Hello, Miss Popover. She hates you. **MORAL:** *Listen.*

43. *Confounding Miss, Mrs., or Ms.* Miss Thinlip, she says clearly. You're not listening. You get up. Hello, Mrs. Thinlip. She hates you. **MORAL:** *Listen.*

44. *Not Suggesting Recesses.* It is prudent to suggest frequent recesses. The jurors who are elderly will bless you.

Well, those are some of the common blunders that defeat has taught me. I'm sure there are hundreds of others that your experiences have suggested to you. I don't know whether this chapter will ever help anyone except maybe some reformer trying to abolish jury selection as a form of voodoo practiced by a dying cult called trial lawyers. But what may happen one day is that you will go to Court to try a case and the jury will vote for you. Then you will be tempted to believe, as we all do, that everything we do is perfect.

Chapter 2

OPENING—
THE TWENTY-SEVEN STEPS

"The beginning is half of the whole."

—Plato

"The first blow is as much as two."

—George Herbert

"Every beginning is hard."

—German proverb

I N SHAW'S *PYGMALION*, HENRY HIGGINS BOASTS THAT HE CAN teach a Cockney flower girl to speak like a lady. He does.

I once heard an old master trial lawyer boast, "I can teach anybody to open. Cross-examine—no! Open—yes!"

I agree. Opening is a learnable art. Here are the twenty-seven steps I try to climb.

1.   *Put Down Your Notes.* College and law school have probably ruined you. You cannot think, stand or talk without notes. However, if you look at your notes, you cannot look at the jurors to study their reactions. How can they have confidence in advocates who read their notes?

> *"Excuse me, jurors, I wish to look at my notes.*
> *I have a further thought—oh yes, here it is—*
> *I wanted to say—my client is innocent."*

Don't be afraid of mistakes in phrasing. Little we say is immortal anyway. Be as natural with the jury as you are in conversation. You're not dull when you converse and you do not use notes when you converse. I know: It is not easy to put our notes down. They are our crutch. Put them down. You will not fall.

2. *Talk as If You Are a Human Being.* Remember life before law school. We said "loss of money," not "pecuniary detriment." The jury will not thank you for saying "testamentary capacity" when you might have said "sound mind and memory."

Sometimes, of course, we may want to anticipate the charge and use a legal phrase. But other than that, we should take our openings and scrub them clean of every vestige of lawyer talk. Remember: Before we were lawyers, we were human beings.

3. *F.D.D.S.* Follow the Dos and Don'ts of Summation (see Chapter 5 on "Summation"), including but not limited to: 1. Don't Start Slowly. 2. Don't Be an Encyclopedia. 3. Speak Anglo-Saxon.

4. *Use Small Words.* Big thoughts do not big words need.

WRONG: "I must satisfy many commitments before I terminate my activities."

RIGHT: "I have miles to go before I sleep." R. Frost

5. *Find Another Description.* All twentieth-century trial lawyers describe the opening as either "the pieces of a puzzle" or "the index" or "the road map" or "the preview of coming attractions." If you can think of a new description, you will be rated with Cicero in legal history.

6. *Stop Belittling the Opening.* Don't tell the jury that "the opening isn't evidence" or "what the lawyers say isn't proof." The Judge will do that gleefully and frequently. Better it would be for you to persuade the jury that every word you utter is gospel truth. Let them know you will never deceive them.

Too often, the trial is over after the opening. Some say the opening is the most important part of the trial. Don't belittle it.

7. *Make Them Trust You.* My favorite opponent is J. Roland Shifty. His eyes dart from side to side as he secretively slides his papers so no one can see them. He never talks. He only whispers furtively. He fulfills the jury's worst stereotyped expectation of the devious lawyer.

Jurors from birth have been taught that lawyers are untrustworthy. Therefore, as an antidote, we must, by every word, by every gesture, communicate our dedication to fair play. The lawyer, by virtue of his or her considerable participation in the trial, has been called the "chief witness." If counsel cannot be believed, the case is probably lost.

8. *Make Them Respect You.* Ms. Paratus has diligently prepared her opening. She has mastered every detail of the death of her client's husband. She begins. However, juror number 4, Miss Lightly, is not listening. Miss Lightly is looking playfully at her new engagement ring. Miss Lightly has little confidence in lawyers anyway.

Ms. Paratus perseveres. She controls her anger. She persists in telling the story of this man's unnecessary death. The facts are technical and detailed and Ms. Paratus has molded them with great care into an impressive statement.

What's this? Miss Lightly now starts to listen. She grudgingly concedes that this lawyer knows what she is talking about. She starts to respect her. Moral: Even an arrogant and frivolous juror can be made to listen.

9. *Win It in Opening.* Larry Limpley, an older lawyer, rarely wins. His openings, tame and timid, seldom stir a soul. He is from the old school. In opening, he merely tells the jurors to keep an open mind. The problem is that the other lawyer, Mr. Kill, isn't waiting. Limpley is fiddling, while Kill is burning with ardor and purpose.

We must try to win it in the opening. The minds of the jurors will never be more open to persuasion. We can't wait too long. If we save everything for cross-examination, we may never be able to catch up.

Therefore, an opening should be the strongest possible statement that is safe. Strong and safe—those are the key words. We cannot be reckless promising that which is undeliverable. That is not safe. We will be castigated in summation for unfulfilled promises. How can we be both strong and safe? By carefully reviewing all depositions, all witnesses' statements, and our investigation file. Know what we've got. Choose words carefully. Then let it rip. It can be done. Making it safe and strong is not contradictory. It is the essence of crafting a good opening.

10. *Be Factual.* Quentin Quarrel constantly argues in opening. Opponents constantly object and Courts constantly sustain. Worst of all, jurors are not persuaded. They know Mr. Quarrel is an advocate. They don't want his conclusions. They want facts. They want to reach their own conclusions.

> **WRONG:** "This manufacturer ignored the well-being of workers."

> **RIGHT:** "This power press crushes with the force of twenty tons. The operator feeds the machine under the press with his hands. This manufacturer never put guards on this machine to prevent hands from being placed under the press."

Openings are like appellate briefs. State the facts properly and you may have already won the argument.

11. *Be Specific.* Generalizations lack life and are not memorable.

> **WRONG:** "John was grievously injured."
>
> **RIGHT:** "They could not save John's leg."

12. *Be Brief.* Openings should be strong, not long. Say not a word more than is needed. Have a reason for saying it or don't say it. Strong, silent types are more interesting than those that blabber endlessly.

13. *Be Selective.* Each case consists of a multitude of facts. Bad lawyers waste time on tangents. Good lawyers are selective. Great lawyers sniff out decisive issues as relentlessly as a dog its bone.

14. *Use the Magic Words.* Judge Purist is a Tartar. "Don't argue in your opening, counselor." "Don't give your opinion, counselor." He never waits for objections. He just rules and rules. Solution: use the magic words with Judge Purist. Preface your key remarks with: (1) "We intend to prove" or (2) "The evidence will show" or (3) "We will learn." This is something of a bending of our advice to talk like a human being. But with Judge Purist, it is wise to bend a bit.

15. *Don't Promise a Witness by Name.* Mr. Pledge, an incautious lawyer, opens to the jurors, "We'll have Dr. Frankincense himself here to tell you that the blood on the machine is my client's." That night, Dr. Frankincense tells Mr. Pledge, "I've been looking at those slides again; I now think that the blood on the machine is not your client's." Oh, Death, where is thy sting, or how do I settle this case? **MORAL:** *Don't promise the names of the witnesses who will give the facts; just promise the facts.*

16. *Don't Be an Ostrich.* If there's a problem, tell the jury. If you don't, your opponent will. Mr. Righteous, an acerbic defense lawyer, loves to open last. It's his summation. He starts with "Now, let me tell you what they didn't tell you." He prays that plaintiff's counsel will not reveal the prior accident or the criminal conviction. He wants to tell them with pious indignation. SOLUTION: *You tell them.*

17. *Motivate the Jury.* Make them want to find for you. Find the noble theme. "Patrick, confined to a wheelchair, has not stayed home. He has found work. He has not quit. He wants to be his own man." Theme: Patrick is no quitter.

18. *Prepare Them for the Evidence.* Use the opening to prepare the jury for evidence that might arouse disfavor. For example:

(1) *Film of Injury.* Some jurors resent any demonstration of injury. Plaintiff's counsel might mention his duty to describe "what happened" to Tom and what "every day of his life is like" and that we have a "brief film." Of course, make sure Judge Strict has already agreed it's admissible.

(2) *Multiple Depositions.* Reading many transcripts can cause jurors to squirm with tedium. You can tell them how time will be saved by examinations before trial, which have the same weight as if a person were on the stand.

(3) *A Hard Cross-Examination.* Not every juror appreciates a fierce onslaught against a witness. Try to prepare them. "We've been told Dr. Smooth will testify for the defense. He has testified many times—for the defense. We look forward to discussing Pat's injury with him which he found not too severe in his one visit of about eighteen minutes." Caution: This is a technique for the seasoned.

19. *Set the Stage.* Mr. Thoughtless leaps in his opening to the very issue to be decided. "We'll prove these doctors damaged the cord between L-2 and L-3." No one knows what he's talking about. What cord? What's L-2? He never explained the anatomy of the spinal cord. He didn't set the stage.

We must never forget the jury. Give them a proper introduction to the facts. It's really an opportunity. Jurors love physical facts. You can feel their resistance soften when you explain the physical facts, be it of an intersection or a construction site. Jurors may not trust lawyers but they trust solid, neutral physical facts.

20. *Foreshadow.* The late, great trial lawyer, François Thespian, was unexcelled in the art of foreshadowing. He created suspense in the opening out of the most ordinary materials. "I tell you, as the plane is about to crash, remember the number '5.' Keep '5' in mind. It is crucial. I'll return to it." His hand would be held high with 5 fingers extended. Later on, he would trumpet on cross-examination, "You say the gauge was at 5?" Then, somehow in summation the whole case and indeed the history of the world revolved about the fact that the "gauge was at 5. I said 5!"

21. *Make Them Remember.* Ours is a manipulative art. We want jurors to remember what we want them to remember. Listen to how Thespian made a jury remember "drinking."

> *"He had a special drink. He would first take a small glass of whiskey, then follow that with a large glass of beer. They call that a-ah-ah. . . ." Juror number three, Mr. Truckdriver, is almost falling off his chair trying to say in a loud stage whisper "Boilermaker." "Oh, yes," says Thespian, "boiler-maker, boiler-maker, they call it."*

22. *Rehearse.* Compared to summation, there is time to rehearse the opening. It is not unlike writing an appellate brief where the record is frozen. We can rehearse openings. That's why, perhaps, there should be more great openings.

23. *Order the Opening.* Tell the reporter at the outset you want your opponent's opening. Even Mr. Cautious may make a mistake and we can use it in cross or summation. In any event, it restrains even our most exuberant adversaries when they know every word of their opening will be read by the enemy.

24. *Tell a Story.* Summation needs an outline to give it meaning. In opening, the form is the story. We answer the question, "What happened?" There may be a few stories: the story of Billy who is dead; the story of the airplane engine that failed; the story of the family he left behind. Story telling—an ancient art, the beginning of all literature—satisfies deep human needs. Stories, well told, can even captivate children. Perhaps a good story can even help us hold the attention of Mr. Macho, juror number two, who truly only wants to think about his mortgage or Monday Night Football.

25. *Be Imaginative.* Mr. Bland is utterly predictable. His openings begin at the beginning and end at the end. Maybe, perhaps, sometimes, it's wiser to start in the middle or even at the end.

> *"Today, Mary Ann lives in a room that she never leaves. She does not see. She does not hear. She does not understand. This trial is the story of how she got that way."*

26. *Save Something.* "The defendant left his home but he made two stops before the fatal crash. We'll ask him about that." You don't yet identify the two stops as being "the One For the Road Tavern" and "the Last Stop Saloon." You save that for cross-examination.

27. *Don't Puff.* It is considered bad form to overstate your position in opening. You may have to eat your inflated words.

EXCEPTION: When you're close to settlement, you can pour it on a little bit. This is the famous "Settlement Opening Gambit." Once when the parties were close to settlement, plaintiff's attorney in opening described her client's injuries most vividly. Juror number five, a burly bartender, became weak and fainted. A recess was called. The defendant found a little more money and the case was settled. **MORAL:** *If you're close to settlement, try to get a juror to faint.*

CONCLUSION:

By telling a story, by not arguing, by weaving facts into an artful theme, the opening can be more persuasive than the most ardent of summations.

The opening is perhaps the most pleasurable part of a trial. Unlike summation, the pressure of victory or defeat is not yet upon us. We are free to enjoy the practice of our uncertain craft.

DIRECT EXAMINATION—
THIRTY-ONE
PERTINENT POINTERS

"Questions are never indiscreet. Answers sometimes are."

—Oscar Wilde

All interrogatories must, to some extent, make a suggestion to the witness. It would be perfectly nugatory to ask a witness if he knew anything about nothing."

—Lord Longdale

D IRECT EXAMINATION, DISDAINED BY TEXT WRITERS AND ignored by students, is the orphan of trial strategy. Cross-examination, celebrated and glorified, is the favorite of trial seminars. If cross-examination is the art of destruction, direct is the art of construction. And for those who must build cases or defenses, direct has much to offer. May I suggest thirty-one pertinent pointers.

1. ***Look and Listen.*** A good direct is a conversation. But not for Mr. Oblivious. His head is in his notes. Every question has been written in advance. He barely looks at the witness. The witness anxiously looks at him for a reassuring smile. But Oblivious is oblivious. He never looks or listens. He hears no shading. He sticks to the stilted script. Mr. Distractor, his opponent, delights in objections that aren't in the script. Mr. Oblivious, distracted by objections, cannot find his place.

Compare Mr. Relaxed. He merely glances at a checklist. He looks at the witness and comforts the witness. Communication is not by words alone. He listens. He does not hesitate to go where the answer takes him. He talks to the witness. It looks like nothing is happening. He's just trying to get the story. In this benign atmosphere, objections make Mr. Distractor look like a rude obstructive bumpkin. **MORAL:** *Look and listen.*

2. *Study the Audience.* Ms. Blind never looks at the jury. She tends to be aloof. She acts as if she's trying the case to a computer, assuming that whoever scores the most points wins.

Ms. Radar looks at the jury but discreetly. She senses every smile and feels every grimace. Her direct examinations respond to every nuance.

The jury is not a computer. Given the same case, Ms. Radar does better than Ms. Blind.

3. *Start Easy.* Some witnesses look upon the witness chair as an electric chair. They even look blank when asked their name. That wasn't covered in preparation.

SOLUTION: Don't begin with anything too hard. Get them to relax. Suggest they sit back and talk up so that all the jurors can hear. Once they get past their name, address and age, perhaps they may be ready for a tough question like "When were you married?". . . . Maybe.

4. *Ask Simple Questions.* Behold Mr. Convoluted. Arms akimbo, sweat on his brow, he gives birth to each question with the most prodigious effort. He specializes in the quadruple negative even on direct. "Isn't it undeniable, that you never, that is, hardly ever, analyzed, during the first week, that portion of the specimen which. . . ." His questions rarely end; they just drift off. Witnesses stare desperately at him in search of his meaning.

Opponents don't even object. They prefer to watch Convoluted sink in the quagmire of his own question.

Contrast Mr. Deft. He uses few words. He makes it look easy. He knows the three greatest questions ever asked on direct. (1) "Who?" (2) "When?" (3) "Where?"

5. *Use Plain Words.* J. P. Dantic adores ornate and pretentious language. For every dimwitted juror foolishly impressed, there are five properly alienated. Many jurors have limited education. Some words are unfamiliar to them. Therefore, use plain words, such as "before," not "prior"; "after," not "subsequent"; "car," not "vehicle."

6. *Get Off Stage.* Counsel is center stage during jury selection, opening, cross and summation. Now you have a good witness. Get off stage. Drift to the rear of the jury box. You and the jurors together, in pursuit of the truth, will listen to the story. If the witness is a disaster, you will, of course, reappear just as the beleaguered prompter comes to the rescue of the actress who forgot her lines. (Please forgive this inapt analogy, which the detractors of the trial bar will cite as evidence of our theatrical nature.)

7. *Use Your Words.* Why concede the other party's language? I like prosecutors who say "robbery," not "alleged robbery." I like plaintiffs' attorneys who say "the day Tom was killed," not "the day in question."

8. *Be Organized.* Mr. Aimless wanders from subject to subject. First, he asks about the weather, then the stairs, the weather, the complaint, stairs, weather, complaint. The jury loses confidence that any subject has been covered. Tennis has been played with their minds.

Ms. Purposeful knows she has four subjects to cover. She covers one and goes logically to the next. Sometimes she'll even announce the next topic. "Let me now ask about the weather. . . ." Have mercy on the jurors. Some of them really do listen to the testimony.

9. *Be Humble.* Take the onus off the witness who is confused by the question.

> **WRONG:** "You didn't understand me?"
>
> **RIGHT:** "I didn't make myself clear?"

10. *Leave Nothing to Chance.* Mr. Haphazard leaves everything to chance. Witnesses testify in no particular order. Whoever happens to be in the corridor will do. Opponents love Haphazard. They know he's good for one unnecessary witness a trial who gets destroyed on cross.

Not Mr. Calculate. He selects, he arranges, he knows that every little point is important. We never know when a juror decides. It is a cumulative process. Therefore, every point is important. Mr. Calculate tries to start and finish every witness with a strong point. He tries to start and finish every day and every trial with a strong witness. He structures the order of witnesses as carefully as a mason builds a monument.

And he always remembers to:

11. *Bury the Cadavers.* Mrs. Spyte, the plaintiff, is ninety-two years old. Everyone expects her to be a sweet, magnificent, grandmotherly witness. In truth, she's the most bitter, vindictive human being you've ever met. She denounces her sainted seventy-year-old daughter as an "ungrateful wimp" because the tea was three minutes late. Mrs. Spyte challenges you, her own attorney, "How do I know you're a lawyer?"

What do you do? Put her on at three o'clock. Hopefully, the jury will be a bit tired after lunch. Leave enough time for cross so she doesn't carry over to the next morning. "The ordeal would be too much for her to return, you know." Have a very short direct. Prove her complaints through nurses, therapists, nieces, nephews—anybody but her. She is a witness to be buried.

If, however, she truly is a sympathetic, grandmotherly type, raise her to a position of honor. Make her the first witness of the day when all are alert and expectant. Linger over the direct. It is a time to enjoy, not to rush. It is a time to give thanks—you have found a strong witness.

12. *Avoid Objections.* We want no distractions. The only problem is Mr. Burst. He always objects. When asked his grounds, he invariably replies, with an originality that would startle Wigmore, "Incompetent, Immaterial and Irrelevant." When pressed for greater particularity, he usually and furiously adds, "Leading, very leading." Leading makes him very angry.

We should try to give Mr. Burst little chance to erupt. Keep the questions simple and the story interesting. Announce, on preliminary matters, "I'll lead here, Your Honor, with your permission." No one can completely silence the Bursts of this world but we should try to avoid objections, particularly legitimate objections brought about by our own thoughtlessness.

13. *Keep It Short.* Ms. Purposeful doesn't ask unnecessary questions. That would hurt her credibility. She doesn't ask forty questions to make four points. That would be inefficient. Every question, every gesture is imbued with purpose. Since something is always happening, she is never dull.

Keeping it short gives the enemy less of a target for cross.

Some students of our art believe witnesses have to win the war on cross anyway. Get them safely and quickly through direct and let the battle begin.

14. *But Be Complete.* Don't omit an essential just to achieve brevity. Prove the prima facie. Prove the suffering. Don't save a "must." Mr. Crafty, your opponent, may be clever and omit it on cross. Judge Technical may not permit it on redirect. Short but complete is not inconsistent, it is the essence of a good direct.

15. *Study Walter Kerr.* Mr. Kerr, the renowned drama critic of past years, often chastised playwrights for placing their best scenes off stage. We are not shown the action. We are only told about it. Mr. Kerr wants the audience to "see" the drama.

A trial is largely a description of past action. But sometimes we can legitimately bring drama into the courtroom. Don't just have the paraplegic with partial use of her arms describe her problems. Show them. "Please button your jacket!" "How do you use that hook to tie your shoes?" "Show us how you strap the knife to your hand when you eat." Each action is accomplished by slow, painful exertion. There is no possibility of feigning. This is dramatic, not theatrical. There has been no overreaching for sympathy. This young woman must do these painful things every day of her life. The jury can bear to see it once. They, themselves, are now witnesses to her suffering.

16. *Prepare.* Mr. Busy prepares all his witnesses in the corridor of the Courthouse. He can be seen outside Trial III every morning "horseshedding" a witness in an area called "Busy's Corner." On the stand, his witnesses are confused. During the brief preparation, Mr. Busy used leading questions to discuss the case. "You were there from four to ten?" The witness in preparation merely had to nod "yes." In the Courtroom, the witness has to talk—an activity for which she is ill prepared. Busy really doesn't know the people he calls to the stand. They are strangers to him. Valuable information has not been mined. Circumstances force all trial lawyers to prepare some witnesses in the corridor, but with Busy it's the rule.

Mr. Busy would like to spend more time with witnesses but he can't. He is busy in too many ways: socially, politically, philanthropically, Bar Associations, investments, his daughter's coming out, his son's coming in. He boasts "I give everything to trial work between nine and five but nights and weekends are mine." That's the talk of a loser. Our best work is done at nights and on weekends. The world of trial lawyers is too competitive. The young ones are coming up consumed with a need for victory. They'll spend the time. They love to beat older lawyers that success has made soft.

All I am laboring to say is: the secret ingredient of preparation is "time."

17. *Ask the Hard Question.* We all shy away from the unpleasant. With each witness, there may be an area of danger. Some lawyers touch it lightly in preparation hoping it will go away. That's wrong. Nothing ever goes away.

Some lawyers are truly superior in preparation. They ask the hard question: "Did you know there were explosives in your basement?" "You did nothing?" "Why?" Find the best answer that exists, ethically and truthfully, and present it as persuasively as possible. That's what advocates do.

18. *Make It Your Best Point.* In preparation, your worst point becomes apparent. Don't turn away. Think on it. The great trial lawyers seem to have a special quality. They are bold. They think about their worst point and sometimes make it their best point.

Mr. Audacity's client was drunk. He doesn't hide it. He proclaims it on direct and prepares for summation: "Tom was dead drunk. Only the motorman had the last clear chance to save this helpless creature."

19. *Know the Magical Question.* Knowledge is the reward of preparation. Mr. Furious is your "notice" witness. In talking to him at his home the night before he testifies, you notice he explodes every time you mention the janitor. It's magical—whenever you say "janitor," he explodes. When he testifies, you take him to a high point and ask, "Mr. Furious, did you tell the janitor?" "Did I tell the janitor? Let me tell you. . . ."

20. *Anticipate the Chestnuts.* You may not believe it, but some cross-examiners are still asking "Did you ever talk to anyone about this case?" And, extraordinary to relate, Mr. Littlehead, your client, is still answering "No." This despite the fact that you spent last week eating, drinking, thinking and doing nothing but talking about the case with Littlehead. We must remember to advise Littlehead that lawyers, at least in the United States, are still permitted to talk to their clients.

21. ***Don't Forget "Lecture 32-A."*** For us, the Courtroom is a familiar workshop. For witnesses, the Courtroom is a strange new world inhabited by odd creatures. They don't know the rules. Give them Lecture 32-A.

"When you're within a block of the Courthouse, you're 'on.' The jury's watching you. Cross at the green. Sit quietly in the Courtroom. Don't sneer at the other lawyer. When your name is called, don't collapse. It's your chance to tell your story. No, don't hold your hand limply when taking the oath. Sit up. Feet on the ground. Please don't slouch. No, no, don't put your arm on the back of the witness chair. Arrogant, you know. It's not only what you say. It's how you say it. Don't look shaken. Cross-examiners are paid to look like they're scoring. Don't be intimidated by his voice. Answer in a polite but firm voice. Be respectful to the Judge. If you don't understand him, smile nicely anyway. Look at the jury on important answers. Eye to eye. Liars can't go eye to eye. Don't overdo looking at the jury. It looks rehearsed. Don't look at me when the other lawyer questions you. It looks like you're searching for the answer. Say 'yes'; it's your answer in the deposition. I'll be reading it to make sure he reads it right. No sarcasm. Pleasant but firm, that's the ticket. Try for humility. I know—that's hard for you. Try for sincerity. I know—that's hard for you. Please try. Etc., etc."

22. *Anticipate Cross.* Mr. Aloof rarely prepares his witnesses for cross. He rather admires those English barristers who upon receiving briefs from solicitors are rarely sullied by excessive intimacy with clients. Cross, however, comes as a rude shock to Aloof's witnesses. The problem is Mr. Brute. He has been trained not in a barrister's chambers but in the trenches of Small Claims Court. Brute loves to cross-examine, particularly those not prepared for his earthiness. He shocks, he shouts, he bullies, he is molten lava and melts many a witness.

SOLUTION: Anticipate cross. (1) On direct, you develop your client's prior conviction or accident. Leave nothing to the Brute. (2) In preparation, shout louder and meaner than the Brute. Make the Brute seem gentle by comparison.

23. *Don't Faint.* Your witness, Dan Dumb, is thoroughly prepared. You approach him with almost a swagger. The entire case depends on your proving it is "blue." You ask with supreme confidence, "What was the color?" Dan Dumb smiles and says "Orange." You titter nervously and say, "I'm talking about the color of the paint. What was that color?" "Orange." Three or four further subtle sallies on your part cause a repetition of the disaster. Your pulse is breaking speed records. Your shirt is wet. You want the courtroom floor to open and swallow you. At moments like this, you know you should have been an actor or an explorer. You consider fainting. No. It is against the rules to faint. You pull yourself together and smile knowingly. You imply that your case has been immeasurably aided by Dumb's surprise testimony. You hint that you'll explain the hidden significance later. To yourself, you pray the settlement offer isn't withdrawn. Since these disasters happen frequently it is important we train ourselves not to faint. It is considered bad form.

24. *Use an Interpreter.* When an interpreter is legitimately needed because of your client's very broken English, do not hesitate to employ one. Why? Some of the happiest moments of my life have been spent watching my opponents turn purple as they try to cross-examine through an interpreter.

25. *Use Visual Aids.* In the television age, we should seek out demonstrative evidence. Jurors love it. Show them pictures, blowups, aerial views, models, the shoe, the machine, the automobile.

But please don't surprise your witnesses with an exhibit they've never seen. Or they may surprise you.

> **Q.** *Please put an X on the photograph showing your coat!*
>
> **A.** *That's not my coat.*
>
> **Q.** *(Nervously) If I may, Your Honor, what's this?*
>
> **A.** *That's not it. That's a fake. Judge, this is a fake.*

Many trial lawyers have run away and now live in Gauguin's South Seas.

26. *Punctuate.* You come to an important question. It should not be submerged in the stream. Punctuate it. Do something different. Move. Sit. Stand. Put down the paper. Pick up the paper. Suggest that something crucial is about to happen. Perhaps announce it. "Please take your time and think back."

Enjoy good answers. Pause. Look meaningfully at a favorite juror without overdoing it. That wizened advocate, Mr. Wily, seems to have a hearing problem after every favorable answer— "Might the reporter please read that back? I didn't quite catch the answer."

27. *Don't Repeat Answers.* Direct by Mr. Unsure:

> **Q.** *When?*
>
> **A.** *Sunday.*
>
> **Q.** *Sunday?*
>
> **A.** *Sunday.*

Q. *Time?*

A. *3 P.M.*

Q. *3 P.M.?*

A. *3 P.M.*

Judge Boyle is now percolating.

Q. *Where?*

A. *Times Square.*

Q. *Times Square?*

A. *Times Square.*

Judge Boyle spills over.

> *Judge:* Mr. Unsure, what's wrong with your hearing?

> *Unsure:* My hearing?

Don't repeat answers. Witnesses may get it wrong the second time. They may think you were dissatisfied with the first answer. The jury may think you're not sure.

28. *But Incorporate.* Counsel receives a favorable answer about "the screeching brakes." The inexperienced might ask: "Did you say the brakes were screeching?" The seasoned advocate asks: "Where were you when the brakes were screeching?"

Mr. Inexperienced repeats; Mr. Seasoned incorporates.

29. *Be Careful with Redirect.* Why give the cross-examiner one more chance to ask the damaging question forgotten the first time? Why act as if the cross hurt? Trial lawyers don't only make points, they make impressions.

Of course, sometimes redirect is necessary to correct an unfair misimpression. Often we can reassert our position, particularly when the cross was way off the mark and a few questions will show it. Redirect can be an opportunity to boldly and briefly capsulize our case. Redirect is a matter of judgment. The experts tell us to keep it short.

30. *Beware of Narrative Questions.* Harry Gair said that direct is the "art of producing an interesting narrative in a simple and persuasive manner."

Yet, the trial bar has a fear of the narrative question, such as "In your own words, tell us what happened." There's no control over the answer. The crucial information, e.g., "the gun was missing," may come in the middle of the answer. The crucial information is not highlighted at the end as it would be if we asked specific questions. The cross-examiner might have the witness repeat the narrative answer which, on second telling, might yield a deviation. And, we worry, ironically, that it may sound rehearsed.

Yet a trustworthy witness can sometimes respond to a narrative question with a natural, obviously uncoached answer that is most persuasive.

Use of a narrative question is, of course, a matter of judgment, but the experts tell us to use it sparingly.

31. *Be Understanding.* Every human being has a story. Mr. Dense never seems to find that story. He doesn't like many of his clients. He doesn't know them.

Ms. Empathy does much better. She "learns" her client, be it a large company or a disagreeable person. She digs until she hits the "why."

Understanding clients is the ultimate preparation.

Understand them. Understand their suffering. "Miss Cry, how did you feel when you first looked in the mirror and saw the scar on your face?" Understand their origins. "Mr. Successful, after night school, did you continue to work in the shipping department?" Who are their parents, their brothers, sisters, spouses, children? Know them as human beings. Make them human. Identify.

Only when we are at one with our clients can we truly represent them. We can then say for them what they cannot say for themselves. This is the very essence of being a lawyer. It is pure advocacy.

CONCLUSION:

Cross-examination will continue to fascinate us. There is something in us that loves a good fight. Yet it is direct examination that builds the structure of a case. And sometimes jurors like to come out of the shadows to believe in something—hopefully, our client, our case. Conceiving persuasive and compelling direct examinations is an act of creation that explains the wonder of why many a trial lawyer finds the art of direct deeply satisfying.

FIFTEEN SUGGESTIONS AND FOUR RULES ON HOW TO SURVIVE CROSS-EXAMINATION

"More cross-examinations are suicidal than homicidal."

—Emory R. Buckner

"Truth fears no trial."

—Thomas Fuller

T HE JUDGE NODS AT YOU. "YOU MAY CROSS-EXAMINE, MR. Shakey." Doubts beset you. "I've too many notes. I don't have enough notes. I'm not a great cross-examiner. I'm no Cicero, Darrow or Perry Mason. What would they do? What should I do?"

Please be calm. Only a few are great cross-examiners. Many great trial lawyers, even great orators, falter in cross-examination. It's curious. Intelligence and preparation may not be enough. Cross-examination is clearly the most difficult and least learnable of the challenges facing trial lawyers. That sense of when to sit down, when to push on, the ability to take a punch, to go for the jugular, are the instincts possessed in full only by the gifted.

Yet the rest of us, the mere mortals, burdened with memories of many an unsuccessful cross, must still go about our daily business of trying cases. If we cannot be master cross-examiners, helping our cause with every question, we should at least strive not to harm our cause. And make no mistake about it, cross-examination is dangerous for the lawyer as well as the witness. If we do not break the witness, the witness breaks us. Jurors usually root for the witness. It's David against Goliath and we're Goliath.

SURVIVAL LIST:

Despite that, can we list a few simple, practical suggestions on how to avoid the slingshots of malevolent witnesses? I believe we can. Here's my survival list.

1. *Don't Always Play D.A.* Miss Adelaide Aged, an eighty-year-old witness, has charmed the jury with her wit. The jurors are in love with her. She swears Mr. Crimson was at the scene. Crimson's lawyer, J. Billy Cose, attacks every witness. He divides the world into two categories: his witnesses and perjurers. He charges at Adelaide headfirst on cross. "You're lying, aren't you? When did you first meet the other lawyer? Is he paying your expenses?" The jury is mesmerized; they can't believe this lout passed the bar examination. Like the cross-eyed javelin thrower from ancient Rome, J. Billy Cose isn't very good, but he captures everyone's attention.

It never occurs to J. Billy Cose that Adelaide may not be lying. She may be mistaken. She doesn't see very well. She admits to talking to her grandson at the time of the incident. Why not, after exchanging a pleasantry, ask her, "Were you playing with your grandson? Do you wear glasses? You say you've stopped watching TV because you don't see too well. Oh, thank you for coming to court, Miss Aged."

Sometimes, we must approach a witness with a smile. Sometimes we must feign indifference. And, of course, sometimes we must scowl with anger. There are many roles to play and emotions to employ. Johnny One-Note is a limited lawyer. For every season, there's a mood. For every witness, there's an approach. Each cross-examination is its own adventure. Sometimes we succeed. Sometimes we fail. The search for the key to each cross-examination cannot be reduced to a formula. That's what makes our work fascinating.

2. *Never Let on You're Hit.* Your investigator has assured you that the witness will say "one o'clock." Time is the issue. You confidently ask, "What time did you see them?" The answer comes, "three o'clock." Good grief, "three o'clock" is what the other side claims. The case is over. You want the ceiling to open so you can fly away.

Keep calm. Display no reaction. If possible, smile knowingly. Move with assurance. It helps to be a bit of an actor at a time like this. Ask anything, but ask with aplomb, "Are you talking Eastern Standard Time? Were you actually looking at your watch?" Or, better, change the subject, "When you say you saw them, what were they wearing?"

You may never recover from the answer. Perhaps the case is lost. But if you fail to conceal your devastated reaction, the jurors, who are always studying you, will know it's lost. Maybe other issues will come along. Maybe this answer can be explained. Hang in there. Reinforcements may be on the way. Don't lose the favorable atmosphere surrounding your case; it may be irretrievable. Many are the skills required of trial lawyers.

3. *Don't Quibble.* Mr. Bicker assumes all jurors have advanced degrees in engineering. He pursues witnesses in search of "inches." "You say it was three feet from the corner. Might it have been three feet and four inches?" Then, he argues in summation that under the Euclidean laws of eternal calculus it would be impossible for the sun to shine unless the answer was three feet and four inches.

Or, "You say Mrs. Verdi was wearing a green dress. Are you prepared to swear it was not a pale shade of olive?"

Jurors start to squirm. The Judge can stand it no more. Think of the hours of tedious get-nowhere interrogations the Court has endured. Your case must be weak indeed if you have to pursue these minnows, thinks the jury.

With malicious delight one recalls the day Mr. Bicker relentlessly quizzed a poor, uneducated witness about the location of the front wheels of her car. "Was it eight feet? Was it twelve feet? Was it more to the left?" The witness was beside herself with confusion. Mr. Bicker, smug with confidence, moved in for the kill. With a slight smirk he inquired, "In your own words, tell us where were the front wheels of your car?" She replied, "Mr., you've got to be kidding, they were on the front of the car." The jury roared—they had been waiting for a chance to laugh at this quibbling, insensitive, unfair splitter of hairs. David won. Everybody loves to see Goliath humbled.

If we shouldn't quibble, what should we do? We should:

4. *Go for the Whales.* Seek out the big issues. Forget the minnows. Jurors do not decide cases on a thousand little points. They want to hear what's crucial.

It doesn't mater where the front wheels were, if the driver had too much to drink.

"How long were you at Happy's Bar? What did you drink? How many? Was your speech slurred? Did you make any other stops?" There are no losers in this string of questions.

Go for the big issue, the critical point that will decide the case. You may not win but the jury will neither squirm nor laugh. And at least you won't lose it on cross.

5. *Know Your Goal.* It's human to be distracted but it's a serious flaw in an advocate.

Your client fell from a utility tower to his death. You claim there was no safety net or like device. That's your theory. The witness for the defense talks about its safety program; he argues that the tower was being improperly dismantled; he testifies, on direct, about everything except safety nets.

On cross, we should not be deflected. We go to the only issue that matters. "Were there safety nets under the tower?" "How much do safety nets cost?" "Have you seen safety nets before?" "Where are your safety nets stored?" "What is the purpose of safety nets?" After your cross, everybody should dream of safety nets for two weeks.

6. *Don't Be Afraid of Pure Cross.* You have no deposition of this witness. You have no records or statements. You are in the customary position of a British or Irish barrister who lives in a world of little or no discovery.

If you believe a witness whose testimony fits comfortably within your theory, there is no problem. Suppose, however, you don't believe this witness whose testimony destroys your position. Then this is a Rubicon you must cross. This battle cannot be avoided with artful finesse. All your training and experience in law and life must be summoned to the fray. It is a most fundamental drama: you versus the witness. You've got to be willing to fight.

> *"I submit you never went to your home on New Year's Day. Isn't that the truth?"*
>
> *"I went there, definitely. I went there."*

That's it. The issue is drawn. The whole case depends on whether the witness went to his home. The cross-examiner earnestly believes the witness is lying. Then go for it. Never stop. Pursue and pursue again.

> *"Where did you go before you went home?" "How did you get home?" "Who went with you?" "How long were you there?" "What did you do when you were home?" "Did you speak to anyone?"*

If the story is false, we should have the confidence to believe the truth will out, somewhere, somehow, under our questioning. Conveying as it does your sincere conviction, pure cross is an exciting opportunity for those brave enough to go for it.

7. *Don't Let Go.* You've got the witness. You caught her in a mistake. Take your time. Enjoy it.

> *"You say today it was 'black' but in this statement you said it was 'white.' Correct?"*
>
> *"Did you read the statement?" "That's your signature, isn't it?" "Do you sign false statements?" "Did you discuss 'black' and 'white' with your lawyer?"*

Suppressing all charitable instincts, some, like the Gila monster, never let the victim go. I do not know how many trial lawyers are in heaven.

8. *Use "Pin Down" Questions.* Never let experts talk. If you do, they will retreat into the forest of their learning. So said Harry Gair.

We must control the witness; the witness must not control us.

All too often, one sees a cross-examiner frustrated with a difficult expert with whom he is contending ask in exasperation, "Well, what is the basis for your conclusion?" You asked her, she'll tell you. It will probably take a half hour and she will run over you like a freight train. Never let them talk; pin them down.

RIGHT: "Was the temperature 101 on Tuesday?"

WRONG: "What's the significance of the elevated temperature on Tuesday?"

RIGHT: "Is elevated temperature consistent with infection?"

WRONG: "How do you diagnose infection?"

Make them say "yes" or "no." Use the weapon of leading questions. Ask the Court to make the witness be responsive.

In addition to experts, beware of pleasant garrulous lay witnesses, usually older ethnic types, who are oblivious to the Judge's rulings. They don't even need questions; they just talk and jurors love them.

EXAMPLE:

Q. *"Was it Wednesday?"*

A. *"Let me tell you, Sonny, it was a very bad day and that client of yours after she went through a red light talked very fresh. She's got some mouth on her."*

Oh, I suppose you could move to strike.

How do you cross-examine these wonders of nature? I'll tell you how: gingerly. But at least try "pin down" questions.

9. *Paint Your Picture.* Even the most antagonistic witness can be put to use.

The manufacturer's expert insists that the employer, not the manufacturer, should guard the power press. However, this expert will fully concede that: (1) somebody besides the worker must guard the press, and (2) an unguarded power press is a disgraceful menace to life and limb.

Even in the simplest of cases, the hostile witness can help. Mrs. Decent testifies on direct that your client went through the stop sign. On cross, however, she will admit, if asked, that the intersection was very busy, that your client was first in the intersection, that your client was hurt very badly, that she spoke before she died and was a model of bravery in her last moments. You have painted your picture. We needn't restrict our cross to their point. We may use our imagination.

10. *Don't Be a Showoff.* Mr. Braggart knows a lot about medicine. He's defending a little personal injury case. The offer is $20,000. The demand is $30,000. Plaintiff's doctor testifies about the patient's neck sprain.

Braggart goes to work on cross. He dazzles the jury by discussing the "discogenic," by locating the "radicular" path of pain, by defining a "myelogram" (never taken), by explaining the "articulation" between "C-4-C-5," by expatiating upon on the proximity of the spinal cord to the area of the "lesion."

The jury is genuinely impressed by the performance of this Hollywood-type lawyer who must only defend big cases. Braggart was magnificent. He won the cross.

Verdict: $100,000.

MORAL: *A few more wins like that and Braggart's clients will all be bankrupt.*

11. *Love Collateral Cross.* When we depart from cross on the merits and explore the collateral issues surrounding the interest of the witness, we enter lawyer's country.

This is easy cross. It requires only the sensitivity of when to go heavy and when to go light.

If defendant's medical expert has been fair, giving you, plaintiff's attorney, everything you deserve and the jury is nodding its approval at the witness, it would be the height of stupidity to snarl, "And how much are you being paid?"

However, when that expert has been grossly partisan and is a "regular" on the courtroom circuit, there are a host of questions to establish "bias." The usual litany will do: "Paid? How much? Testify? How often? In thirty-eight states?"

Also consider lay witnesses as candidates for collateral cross. Sgt. Constable is called by the defendant shopkeeper. As he enters the courtroom, you notice he nods ever so slightly to Mr. Merchant, the shopkeeper. Then your opening, "You know Mr. Merchant? How long? Have you spoken about this case?"

This kind of cross is easy because you don't have to know everything to do it. This cross is effective because the jury understands it. They may not comprehend neurological mysteries but they know "money."

12. *Always Ask for Records.* The first question for every expert is "May I see the file you brought with you?" You may hit pay dirt. Remember what Job said: "Would that mine enemy would write a book." MORAL: *Experts should bring only their laundry tickets to the stand.*

13. *Be Yourself.* True for every phase of the trial. Don't imitate anybody, no matter how great. Be natural. But it's hard to be natural. It's only the practiced hand that can make the natural gesture. (Willa Cather, again.)

We have to work at it. We have to trust ourselves. We're all unique.

14. *Be Prepared, Not Rigid.* Many a novice has all the questions for cross prepared in writing. Forget it. The witness will never cooperate. The other lawyer will delight in raising objections to distract the neophyte.

One cannot walk in the narrow aisle of such tight preparation. Of course, we should have a checklist, but we must keep our freedom to go where the answers take us like a good interviewer. We should be conceptual, not clerical.

There's room for many styles. Some movie directors come to filming with a tight script. Others wait for inspiration to descend.

E X A M P L E :

We're prepared to try to extract on cross from the defendant's doctor the admission that depression is permanent. The doctor will not assent to that but in passing mentions that depression is hard to reverse. That's a very valuable admission. The muse will more often reward those who are prepared.

15. *Act Like You're Getting Somewhere.* Great cross-examiners always act as if they're getting somewhere. They start smartly. They finish strong. They exude confidence. They seem to find guilty inferences in every answer, no matter how innocent.

What is truly aggravating is that they may be getting nowhere. Who said life is fair? **MORAL:** *Act like you're getting somewhere.*

FOUR RULES (WITH A "BUT")

1. *Don't Repeat Direct.* This is the most common mistake of the apprentice. The direct covers ABC. The cross covers ABC. All that does is reinforce the direct. Rather, on cross we should go for what wasn't covered on direct. Sometimes they don't cover what they're afraid of.

On direct, they never asked their own janitor about prior complaints. Go for it. Of course, we must be wary of traps. I said, "Don't repeat direct." But there's an exception: make a witness repeat a pat rehearsed statement to establish its falsity.

For example, when the defendant's construction foreman who has an eighth-grade education says, "We had a perfect safety record neither blemished nor tarnished by prior incident and therefore we were never on notice of a dangerous condition," please have him repeat that.

2. *Don't Be Long.* Everybody knows the first rule of cross is to sit down. "No questions" can be very effective. Don't ask more questions than you must.

But we all know of witnesses who enthrall jurors at first. It takes time to discover their true nature. Mr. Pharmacist was upright, splendid and impeccable for the first two days of cross. After a lengthy and sustained review of all his records by the plodding cross-examiner, Mr. Pharmacist finally admitted he changed the records of the prescription prior to the lawsuit.

Occasionally, it takes time to capture the quarry.

3. *Don't Ask Why.* That's elementary. That's like asking an enemy expert for his reasons.

But sometimes when the witness is cornered there is no better question. First, we must make sure all escape routes are tightly closed. "Why didn't you come to the emergency room when called?" It was known that the doctor wasn't operating and that he wasn't busy, but it was also known that he wasn't there because he had a personality conflict with the nurse in the E.R. Why, indeed, didn't he come?

"Why" can be a great weapon, but perhaps it's best left to the more experienced hunter.

4. *Don't Be Nasty.* A soft word turneth away wrath. A smile can disarm the most hostile witness. Be courteous and fair to all witnesses and by your decency carry the jury with you. I believe these sentiments and try to practice them.

But I must admit that some bristling nasty cross-examiners are stupendously successful. They know when to pounce and when not. These Tartars thrive on nastiness. Some would say they couldn't be anything but trial lawyers. And, jurors, perhaps bored with their own lives, love it. **MORAL:** *No rule is absolute.*

The judge calls again, "Mr. Shakey, are you ready to cross-examine?"

Shakey rises and with cool disdain stares at the witness. "Mr. Exaggerator, do you mean to tell me that. . .?"

SOME DOS
AND DON'TS
FOR SUMMATION

WE SIT IN A COURTROOM LISTENING TO A SUMMATION. Suddenly, we find ourselves squirming. The jurors are yawning. The judge nods but tries to appear profoundly concerned. Opposing counsel is gleeful. What is wrong? While one may not be able to "win it" in summation, it certainly seems one can "lose it" in summation. Some veterans will tell the neophyte "don't" do that but "do" do this. I've tried to prepare a list of some of the simple dos and don'ts of summation as overheard around the courthouse corridors.

1.   *Don't Start Slowly.* Mr. Ponderous arises with great solemnity to issue his closing oration. He straightens his vest, adjusts his spats and pulls on his watch chain. He takes three sentences to say his summation is not evidence. He takes two more sentences to apologize for sundry misdeeds, clears his throat three times, and starts his summation. But it's too late. The jury is gone.

Television has changed our jurors for all time. When Presidents speak they are given at most thirty seconds on the evening news. Headline stories get ten or fifteen seconds. What do the viewers do when they are bored? They change the channel.

Certainly there's time to say "thank you" or exchange a pleasantry but we meander ponderously at our peril. **MORAL:** *Capture them quickly.*

2.   *Don't Be an Encyclopedia.* Mr. Eternal steps to the lectern. Out come his notes. They are in two volumes, two feet thick. He has one and a half feet of daily copy. He will read most of it. The jury shudders. They know they're in for it. It's going to be a three-hour speech after a two-day trial.

We shouldn't read back the entire record. We should be making an argument. We should be selecting and arranging the evidence to support our points.

We don't have to review the testimony of every witness to describe the history of a power press. To make a pointed summation we merely have to show: (1) the enormous potential for damage to the user, and (2) the manufacturer's indifferent failure to guard this dangerous machine.

One novelist enters a room, records everything and becomes an encyclopedic bore. Another enters the same room and selects only one or two details, but vividly brings the scene to life.

3.   *Don't Use Jargon.* Don't say "voir dire." Is that a French restaurant? Don't say "This is a *res ipsa* case." Do some lawyers charge more for Latin? Don't say "This is a blind accident." Does that mean someone is without sight?

4.   *Speak Plainly.* Mr. Pedantic loves big words. He always says "ecchymosis" rather than "black and blue." But for every dimwitted juror who falls for it, there are five jurors who are too smart to be impressed. Big words and fancy phrases do further harm by drawing attention from the case to the lawyer. We want the jury to see us not as great lawyers with a poor case but rather as poor lawyers with a great case. We must speak plainly but without condescension. We are communicators.

5. *Speak Anglo Saxon.* Say "graveyard," not "cemetery." Say "hurt," not "injured." Say "wrong," not "tort." Say "dead," not "deceased." Say "widow," not "surviving spouse."

6. *Use the Language of the Charge.* Plaintiff's attorney, when pleading for the right of a child to recover for the death of her father, should use the word "nurture," because the Court is going to use the word "nurture." The charge will then ring a bell in the minds of the responsive jurors.

Tell the jury that the failure to guard the machine was the "'cause,' what we call the 'proximate cause'" of the mangled hand. The Court will use the phrase "proximate cause" in its charge. It will enhance your credibility.

Tell the jury your evidence certainly "tips the scales." Most judges in civil cases advise juries that plaintiff's evidence must "tip the scales, no matter how slightly, to prevail."

Whenever you can properly do so, use the language of the charge. We do not trespass upon the Court's domain. But certain phrases, of necessity, will appear in the charge. These phrases are available to the advocate.

The jurors, even the cynical ones, are at their most attentive when they turn to the Court at the end of the case to listen to the final instructions. Let the language of the charge serve you.

7. *Don't Give Your Opinion.* Ms. Prosecutor says "I tell you that I have no axe to grind. I am a public servant and in my opinion this defendant is guilty and I wouldn't prosecute him unless I thought he was guilty." That is a guaranteed reversal. What hurts is that this error is easily rectified. All the prosecutor had to say was "The evidence establishes the guilt of the defendant." In that way, felons will not on technicalities go free.

Play within the rules. If Shakespeare wrote his sonnets within the rules, there is no reason why we lesser mortals can't do the same with our summations.

8. *Don't Get Carried Away.* "This wealthy corporation is worth millions of dollars more than my poor client, Mary Pitiful." Judgment for plaintiff reversed.

"I may not be Abraham Lincoln but I'm still entitled to a fee and include that in your award." Judgment for plaintiff reversed.

"This defendant is a man who's used to paying a premium for what he has in life. I assure you he's always in good hands wherever he travels throughout all of this state." Judgment for plaintiff reversed.

I know it's tempting but don't do it.

9. *Use an Outline.* Mr. Chaos believes that the Muse will always strike him. He is vain. He believes that if he merely opens his mouth, the words will flow. He has many good ideas but they never seem organized. When he is making one point, another irrelevant point occurs to him. Sometimes Chaos has the jury mesmerized at the beginning of his argument, but then he starts to repeat himself. The jury, at first sympathetic, starts to wonder. This wouldn't happen if Chaos used an outline. The neophyte lawyer asks: "What's the secret behind having an outline?" It's very simple: You have to prepare. Genius is wonderful but preparation is better.

10. *Don't Answer Their Questions.* Mr. Sly looks at the young plaintiff's attorney and tells the jury that before Mary Smith can recover, her attorney must satisfactorily answer the following thirty-nine questions. The young plaintiff's lawyer dutifully records all the questions and proceeds to answer them one by one. After the last answer, his time is up and his case is over. Antidote: don't answer their questions. Make your own argument. Emphasize your strong points. You should answer only those questions that truly must be answered. You must present your case and not take the bait of a sly opponent.

11. *Don't Be Too Insensitive.* The little old plaintiff, Tim Small, a kindly man who works as a janitor, lost four fingers in the accident. Defense counsel, Mr. Ox, wants to prove that the injury is not overly devastating. He argues: "You know, Mr. Small is a janitor. It's not as if he played the piano and was another Liberace."

I see a very large verdict falling on the Ox.

12. *Don't be Arrogant.* The word "I" should not precede every single sentence in a summation. It is not you but your client that counts. Humility is still the trial lawyer's best friend. We shouldn't take ourselves too seriously. A touch of modesty does wonders. It often melts resistance. It also makes defeat easier to bear.

13. *Don't Use a Weak Argument—Use Imagination.* The plaintiff, Mr. Boozer, was dead drunk and fell on the railroad tracks before the train struck him. Sometimes an inexperienced and less than candid advocate will try to deny that Mr. Boozer had been drinking. The evidence is overwhelming. The jury is offended and throws the case out.

Wouldn't it be better to use imagination? Better to admit the truth, ethically and strategically better, and say: "Of course, Boozer was drunk! Who more than a drunk needs the reasonable care of a motorman who had the last clear chance to avoid the tragedy? Boozer was helpless. Only the defendant's motorman could have prevented the impact." Sometimes with imagination the hardest bit of evidence can become for us the best evidence.

MORAL: *Don't use weak arguments.* They underestimate the intelligence of jurors. It was said of Erskine that he was a great advocate because he did not talk at jurors. Rather he reasoned with them. He gave full weight to the reasonableness of his opponent's arguments. In that way, he was irresistibly persuasive.

14. *Don't Be Greedy.* The liability is weak but the injuries are substantial. You've been reading about those large verdicts. You want one. It will help with "business." You tell the jury that "justice will be served only by a verdict of $2 million." The jurors are deeply troubled. They would like to award something but $2 million is ridiculous. The verdict is for the defendant.

MORAL: *Jurors resent overreaching.*

15. *Look at the Jury.* Mr. Diffident presents a rather logical argument. His summation is well prepared. He is a conscientious lawyer. But his experience has been more in other stages of litigation than in trial work. He does great "paper." His arguments are reasonable, well researched and nicely worded. But his summation lacks life. Why? He's not making contact with the jury. He is treating his summation as if it were part of a high school debate. But a summation is more than a debate. It's the win-or-lose, life-or-death resolution of rights. You had better believe your argument. If you don't, jurors will know it in a second. You've got to look at them.

Also, when you're looking at them you can tell when you're losing them. You can then change your argument. I know of a lawyer who asked the jury for a million dollars and they laughed. The lawyer talked to them. "Will you give me a chance to explain?" Some nodded "yes." He said, that if "cargo or a horse or a painting worth a million dollars was destroyed by someone's fault, you'd award a million dollars, wouldn't you?" Some nodded "yes." The lawyer said, "Well, I'm arguing for a human being." The argument didn't completely succeed but it helped obtain a substantial verdict.

Please look at the jury. Don't look at the floor. There are no voters on the floor.

16. *Don't Think of Yourself.* Mr. Nervous, a young lawyer, upon being given a jury slip, fainted. That's a very bad start.

During his summation, he stood frozen in one spot. He worried how his tie looked; he fretted that his voice sounded strained; he was concerned that his gestures were too awkward.

Intending no immodesty, I believe I know what he's doing wrong and how to correct it. He is thinking of himself—an unworthy preoccupation. He should be thinking of his client and his cause. Lawyers are privileged to be entrusted with the well-being of their fellow human beings.

If we worry only about our client's receiving her fair due, we will never worry about our tie, our skirt, our voice or our gestures. We will be too consumed with our case.

17. *Believe.* Mr. Sincere's summation isn't perfect but there's no fakery in it. He is carried along on the wave of his belief. He has faith in his cause. He has precisely what Virginia Woolf says the great writers possess: "fierce attachment to an idea." Sincere conviction sweeps away many a mistake and is the single most important ingredient in a fine summation.

18. *Have a Little Courage.* The case has not gone well. Juror No. 4 hates us. She turns away every time we speak. The judge disdains our every argument. The client is unhappy with us. All seems lost and it's time to sum up. What should we do? We should disregard our client's hostility. We should sum up like our back is against the wall because it is. There comes a time when we run out of strategies. All the stratagems of our craft will not save us.

We have to fall back on the first attribute of the advocate: character. Without character, we are empty strategists.

A little philosophy helps. Defeat does not result in disbarment or banishment. Our family, our law firm and even the planet will still be there if we lose. There's no shame in defeat—only in not looking Juror No. 4 in the eye.

You, a young lawyer, ask "Do you mean if I follow this list of 'dos and don'ts' I'll always give great summations?" No. But what may happen is that one day you'll give a summation and win the case. Then you'll be tempted to think you know how to do it. You may even be asked to lecture and write columns. And you'll live happily ever after until your next summation when the jurors yawn and the judge nods.

Settlement—Six Villains, Three Heroes, One Play, and Ten Commandments

"An ill agreement is better than a good judgment."
—George Herbert

"It is the duty of a good judge to prevent litigation."
—Old legal maxim

PROLOGUE

CONSIDER A LEGAL SYSTEM WITHOUT SETTLEMENT. ALL CASES go to verdict; all verdicts to appeal. Commerce stalls while advocacy roars. Only two classes exist: lawyers and litigants. Resolving a dispute often costs more than the amount in dispute. Think of Voltaire, who said he went to law twice and lost both times: once when he lost a case and again when he won. And some dear worthies of our profession would love a world without settlement.

SIX VILLAINS

1. *Mr. Bullrump.* John Bullrump, the renowned defense counsel, lives for the trial of cases. It is mother's milk to him. He takes verdicts because he must take verdicts. His therapist notices definite improvement after John discharges a vitriolic summation. John never discusses settlement. With surly contempt for cowardly negotiators, he asserts: "I am a trial lawyer, not an adjuster."

2. *Mr. Love.* Jack Love adores his cases. No client of his has ever done wrong. Every case is worth millions. He rejects regularly the Judge's recommendations for settlement. He loses a lot. You'd think he'd learn. He can't. Let a weakness in his case be revealed and he will conjure up countless excuses. He is a legal romantic condemned to fall in love with every case. Blind to all peril, he considers settlement a betrayal.

3. *Mr. DeSeaver.* Donald DeSeaver gets retained by hook or crook. He promises clients the world. A master of puffery, he outbids other lawyers in getting clients to hire him. Judges can't understand why his clients won't accept reasonable suggestions for settlement. DeSeaver knows. He has bloated their expectations beyond all reason. The case will never settle. DeSeaver doesn't care. He got the case, didn't he?

4. *Mr. Famengreed.* Winston Famengreed lives for fame and money. He wants to be the richest and most famous lawyer in the state—no, the country—no, the world—no, the universe. His public relations firm regularly places him on television and in newspapers. Winston has an opinion on every subject. He craves attention. He was the boy in class who always waved his hand when a slow child tried to answer. He sees every verdict as a headline. He never relays offers to clients. He never settles. He says "Big verdicts get big headlines. Big headlines get more business." His office already has too many cases. Files sit on the floor, fall off desks, gather dust on shelves. Motions to dismiss abound. Underpaid associates groan under the weight of gargantuan caseloads.

And yet Mr. Famengreed advertises for more cases. What does Winston Famengreed want? He wants More, More, More!

5. *T.D.T.* Theodore Perdiem, a defense lawyer, dodges settlement the way burglars dodge the police. He can never find his file. He never has authorization. His principal, when called for money, is always out to lunch. Mr. Perdiem bills by the day. Often on the third day of trial, he gets authorization. They call him: T.D.T.—Three Day Teddy.

6. *Judge Eruditis.* The Honorable Erasmus Eruditis loves judging and hates settling. He sees his holy mission as the unraveling of legal mysteries. In each case, no matter how small, he divines issues invisible to the ordinary mind. Judge Eruditis has been known to instruct a jury for over four hours on a simple case of modest damages which took one day to try. The charge was beautiful, abounding with references to Blackstone. It made the lawyers cry. The case had been near settlement but Judge Eruditis chilled negotiations by refusing to talk to the lawyers. With great humility, he proclaimed "You fellows know a lot more about money than I do." He never talks to lawyers in chambers. He never speaks to each side privately. He never discusses settlement. He is a pure Judge.

THREE HEROES

1. *Ms. DeFender.* Debra DeFender successfully defends cases. She never negotiates out of fear but never fears to negotiate. Fierce in the courtroom, reasonable in chambers, Debra enjoys the confidence of Judges and opponents. A busy practitioner, she never waits three days before settling. Her clients save money. Debra knows the secret of successful defendants' bargaining: offer a little less than the case may be worth but enough to tempt them.

2. *Mr. FitzPlaintiff.* Peter FitzPlaintiff tries a beautiful case. He prepares for verdicts but listens to offers. While he has many cases, his client has but one. Judges and opponents trust Peter. Cases get settled. Peter knows the secret of successful plaintiffs' bargaining: Demand a bit more than the case may be worth but low enough to tempt them.

3. *Judge Listen.* The Honorable Lawrence Listen wants to know the case. He listens carefully to lawyers. He asks questions. He learns the case. He speaks to each side privately. He discourages frivolous positions, acknowledges strong points and by the force of sheer reasonableness extracts sensible positions. The attorneys welcome his suggestions. Unlike a rote-like Solomon, he does not merely split the difference. By listening, he goes where the evidence takes him. His pretrials are the original minitrials. The solution to much of what plagues our Court system can be gleaned from his conferences.

THE BAD CONFERENCE—OR WHY CASES DON'T SETTLE (A PLAY IN ONE ACT)

The Court of Lukewarm Sessions.

ACT I

Judge Eruditis: I guess you people have talked about this case. There's no sense in my trying. (Eruditis never tries. If he doesn't have this case, he'll have another.)

Mr. Bullrump: The case has to be tried. It's a matter of principle. (Bullrump has not had a case in all his time at the Bar that didn't have to be tried because of principle.)

Mr. Love: It can't be settled. My client did no wrong.

Mr. Perdiem: I'd like to settle but the man with the money is out to lunch.

Mr. Famengreed: It can't settle for a penny less than a million dollars. (In thirty years of practice, Famengreed has never had a case worth a penny less than a million dollars.)

Judge Eruditis: There are some fascinating issues here. (He's already starting to get that Oliver Wendell Holmes look in his eyes.)

Mr. Love: How can we agree, Judge? They almost killed my client.

Mr. Bullrump: That's a filthy lie. Do I have to listen to this?

Mr. Famengreed: I can't take less than a million dollars. I was just figuring my fee alone.

Mr. Perdiem: I just called again. The man is still out to lunch.

Judge Eruditis: Let's pick a jury. I think there's a law review article in all this.

THE END OF THE CONFERENCE AND ALL HOPE.

"THE TEN COMMANDMENTS OF SETTLEMENT" (A LECTURE BY JUDGE LISTEN)

1. *Thou Shalt Not Spurn Settlement as Being Beneath Thee.* Don't be Judge Eruditis, who considers settlement a crude rug auction beneath his dignity. Don't be Mr. Bullrump, who must win every case to prove how tough he is. Certainly, prepare every case for verdict and never fear to take a verdict. But also never fear to negotiate. Without settlement, the system of civil litigation in America would collapse.

2. *Thou Shalt Respect Thy Enemy.* Don't be Ms. Obnoxious, who tells her opponent she speaks only to the lead lawyer. Cooperate with staff lawyers—or, for that matter, insurance companies. Send supporting documentation. It's the age of disclosure anyway. They've got a job to do. Help them get their reserves up and their animosity down. Don't have them mark your case in red for warfare because you're obnoxious.

3. *Thou Shalt Treat Thy Client as Thou Wouldst Be Treated.* Don't be Mr. Famengreed, who puffs and exaggerates and predicts great big verdicts in order to get his client's signature on a retainer. Don't be Ms. Incommunicado, who refuses to return clients' phone calls. Keep your client advised of all important events, and of every single offer no matter how puny. Treat your client the way you want your physician to treat you—with understanding and explanations.

4. *Thou Shalt Not Bargain as if Thou Were Born Yesterday.* Don't be Ms. Naive, who makes "off the record" demands that are then inscribed in granite by opponents. Don't be Mr. Suspicious, who won't level with a Judge who's genuinely trying to settle a case. Emulate Mr. FitzPlaintiff, who always starts a bit high but somehow usually works it out with a smile on everyone's face.

5. *Thou Shalt Not Evaluate Each Case as if It Were the Last One in Your Office.* Don't be Mr. Young Lawyer, who demands a million dollars on every case in order to build a big reputation. Don't be Mr. Love, who loves his every case and evaluates it at ten times its true value.

6. *Thou Shalt Know the Law.* Don't be Mr. Ignorant, who hasn't read an advance sheet in twenty years and doesn't know the perils of settling with one co-defendant and continuing against another. Rather be Ms. Prepared. She knows the possible pitfalls of settling with only one defendant and knows the special requirements of settling the case of an infant, an incompetent or a decedent.

7. *Thou Shalt Seek the Counsel of Elders and Experts.* Don't be Mr. Arrogant. Ask the older lawyers what they think of value and strategy. Be Ms. Humble. She asks economists about structured settlements. She asks friends and secretaries what they think of her case and the value of it. Mr. Arrogant is too proud to ask anyone anything.

8. *Thou Shalt Keep Abreast of Modern Ways.* Don't be Ms. Obsolete, who never considers a structured settlement even for a plaintiff who has no ability to deal with large lump sums. Ms. Obsolete doesn't like new ways. She doesn't understand them. She never sends a bad faith letter. She never considers a settlement brochure or a videotape. By not keeping current, she serves clients poorly.

9. *Thou Shalt Not Be a Hero.* Don't be Mr. Olympian, who must make a big score and a big headline on every case. Be Mr. Prudent. He knows his client has only one case, which must be shepherded carefully.

10. *Thou Shalt Think Settlement.* This is the greatest of the commandments since it embraces all the others. It means: be wise. With persistence and imagination, even difficult cases settle. The wise lawyer knows a secret: most cases settle. Lawsuits, like wars, almost all eventually settle. The only question is how many coffins must first be filled.

Living with Experts— Twenty Pungent Proverbs and Eighteen Little Gambits

"An expert is a guy from out of town."

—Anonymous

"An expert is one who knows more and more about less and less."

—Nicholas Murray Butler

"An expert is one who learns more and more about less and less until ultimately he knows everything about nothing."

—Variation

W HO CAN EVER FORGET THE LAST SCENE OF THE MOTION picture "The Good Earth?" Paul Muni saved the crop and his own soul by beating back a plague of locusts. We trial lawyers now have our ordeal. We must learn how to survive the swarms of experts descending upon the courthouses. For those who must learn to live with experts, here are twenty pungent proverbs and eighteen little gambits.

SELECTION

1. ***Professionals Walk Too Many Streets.*** In Greenback County, everybody uses B. B. Hooker. B. B. charges "Big Bucks" but he's worth it. Jurors love him. What sincerity! But there's trouble in Greenback County. Lately, jurors aren't buying B. B. He's starting to sound like a lawyer. "Let me see the photograph deemed in evidence as Exhibit 5A," said Hooker in one case. He gets killed on cross. "I testified forty-three times last year." "I rendered seventy-five reports for lawyers in March." "This is the fourth time I've testified for Mr. Tired." "Most of my income comes from legal consulting work." "I haven't actually worked on a construction site in eight years."

His courtroom manner is a little frayed. He speaks with a bit too much flourish—like an old Shakespearean actor. He has seen better days. Why do they still use him?

It's a familiar tale. Experts like Hooker often start brilliantly. They know their subject. They are articulate. They have a gift for explaining. They enjoy the courtroom. And the money is good. They abandon all and become forensic experts. At first, they are discovered by a few lawyers. Then, word gets around and everybody's using them. Their standards are initially high. Then, somehow, as the years go by, they always seem to say what has to be said. Lawyers still use them because they never let them down. It's easy. Just pick up the phone and they're there. The problem is they are no longer effective. Professionals like Hooker who walk too many streets are no longer desirable.

SOLUTION: Don't be lazy. Eschew the regulars. Find that persuasive "unused" expert who will varnish, not tarnish, your case. Look for the mechanic with dirty hands or the junk dealer with torn coveralls. "Those toasters are no damn good. We picked up five this year after they started fires." Use the Yellow Pages. Find the professor who, if only given the chance, would love to criticize any non-academic human being, particularly one who is successful. Look for scientists employed by government anxious to augment their income. Confer with technical societies. Be imaginative. Dare to ask the most famous author of the most authoritative article to be your expert—because your cause is just. Just don't settle for the old Hooker.

2.   *Amateurs Don't Know the Neighborhood.* Nora Novice, a new lawyer, read somewhere that she shouldn't hire shopworn experts. She retains Tyrone Tyro, a toxicologist who testifies for the first time. Tyrone is untouchable in his pristine purity. No report or testimony has ever soiled his spotless innocence. There is only one problem: Tyrone is an undiluted disaster.

Judge Primo Facio is a purist. Experts must say "reasonable certainty." Mr. Sly cross-examines Tyrone:

> **Q.** *"By reasonable certainty, you don't mean absolute certainty, do you?"*
>
> **A.** *"No. No."*
>
> **Q.** *"In all fairness, Professor Tyro, you'll admit true certainty doesn't exist among eminent scientists such as yourself?"*
>
> **A.** *"You have a point."*
>
> **Q.** *"Science deals with the infinite world of possibilities, does it not?"*
>
> **A.** *"Well put, sir."*

And now, coming in for the kill, roaring in a voice that nobody ever used before to Professor Tyro:

> **Q.** *"And I put it to you, sir, that when you said reasonable certainty you merely meant it was possible and not a jot more?"*
>
> **A.** *(Completely wilting under the unaccustomed heat) "Of course, I only meant it was possible."*
>
> **Q.** *"And that's all any honest scientist could mean?"*
>
> **A.** *"I am an honest scientist, sir."*
>
> **Q.** *"Of course, of course."*

Quandary: If a professional is too "used" and an amateur too "unused," what is the solution? Please read Pungent Proverb 6: "Take an Expert to Dinner."

3.   *Blessed Are They Who Believe.* The greatest attribute in experts is conviction. Once persuaded your cause is just, they are ready.

"It's a sin they didn't put a guard on that blade."

"They didn't shore the trench at ten feet? That's ridiculous. In that soil, they should have shored at eight feet."

"No wonder they couldn't see the metal speck in his eye. In this x-ray, you're lucky to see his eye."

When seeking an expert, find a believer. Being in a courtroom with an uncommitted expert is like being in a foxhole with a noncombatant.

4.   *On a Long Trip Take a Spare Tire.* Professor Ludwig Schreiben, for fifty years Europe's foremost handwriting expert, has agreed to testify for you that the signature on the one billion dollar contract is a forgery. On the eve of trial, he runs away to Venice with his childhood sweetheart and refuses to return. What do you do? If the case is important enough, you should have a backup. Don't put all your experts in one basket.

A spare expert can be used in other ways. Dr. Spare can sit in during trials and depositions to guide you more easily than a testifying expert. Dr. Spare can help you find experts; Spare can be your expert on experts.

PREPARATION

5.   *Preparation Begins at Home.* To prepare the expert, you must prepare yourself first. Larry Lazy meets his neurosurgeon for the first time in the courthouse.

The doctor refers to a "subdural hematoma."

Larry says, "What's that?"

Doctor: "Under the dura."

Larry: "The dura?"

Doctor: "Well, it's a very serious hematoma."

Larry: "Hematoma?"

Would you believe Larry is charging his client for this interview? Larry is lazy and he's a disgrace. He's wasting the doctor's time and his client's money.

What should we do? Prepare first and then meet the expert. Learn the doctor's jargon. Read a book. Take a course. Know more than your opponent. Knowledge is an advantage. And more than that, preparing a case can be fun. Being a lawyer allows us to learn everybody else's business. Larry Lazy doesn't know what he's missing.

6. ***Take an Expert to Dinner and You May Break More Than Bread.*** Go to dinner. The phones won't be ringing. Get to know each other, particularly if the expert's an amateur. Tell your expert the names of the combatants and the issues that divide them. It'll be a warm-up. A trial isn't a high school debate. Get the expert involved. Have you ever noticed that when an expert arrives at court early, she may change from a cold spectator to a warm participant? "Why, the other side's all wrong," she may say, and you'll know she's more than a mercenary.

Start leisurely. Talk generalities at first. There's time enough later to prepare the key questions. Know each other's mind. Read all her records and avoid surprises.

Slowly get more specific. Have her give you a list of every applicable code and regulation. Experts can be instant libraries and provide us with "standards" in the never-ending search for deviation (plaintiff) or compliance (defendant).

Then start to put your direct together and anticipate the cross. Ask the hardest question in the case. You may have to meet a few times. Each time, you will discover more and grow more confident.

Take your time together and you may break the case as well as bread.

POINT: An expert cannot be prepared casually on the phone. With care, we can make the most inexperienced but highly qualified expert into a formidable presence. And even those with forensic experience will benefit from this process. Shortcuts are for losers.

7.   *Dull Teachers Can Learn from Bright Students.* It's not a one-way street. We, the lawyers, can sometimes teach the experts, who in turn are our teachers.

Experts, particularly the inexperienced, don't know the courtroom as we do. Tell your expert that he who hesitates to admit that two plus two equal four is a transparent advocate who does more harm than good. Tell your expert to avoid sarcasm to the other lawyer. A wise lawyer once observed, "Asperity towards a lawyer is a judge's prerogative." Tell the expert to speak simply. To use short sentences. To watch the jury, and if the jurors are bewildered, stop. To recapture their attention with greater clarity. To listen to questions. To be responsive. To not argue. To not play lawyer. To not lose her temper.

Let the expert rehearse. Use videotapes; use other lawyers in the office to cross-examine.

Sometimes we can even teach substance. We may find a helpful article or a report unknown to the expert.

And the greatest accomplishment of all is when you, immersed totally in the subject, can suggest a theory to your expert that rings true. "You're right. That would explain it." If Plato went a step or so beyond old Socrates, surely we can give a pointer or two to our experts.

THE COURTROOM

8.   *Good Lawyers Are Translators.* Most experts speak in the foreign language of their jargon. The chemist has his "benzene ring" and the epidemiologist has her "cohort study," while the immunologists have their "T cells." We must translate. "When you say the road had a grade of three, do you mean that for every hundred feet of length there is an elevation of three feet?" "Would a five cent cup of coffee in 1940 that now costs fifty cents be an example of what you mean by inflation—an inflation of 1,000 percent?"

Many jurors did not have the privilege of an extended education. Good lawyers help them. A good lawyer says, "In the early 1900s" rather than, "In the early Twentieth Century." In the courtroom, every thought we have, every word we say, every breath we draw, every gesture we make is for the jury—whether we are looking at them or not—and particularly when we're not looking at them.

9.   *A Lot of Knowledge Is a Dangerous Thing.* That conscientious advocate, Stuart Stuffed, is crammed full of knowledge. He is filled to the brim with knowledge. Were he to add one more fact, he would burst.

Mr. Stuffed recently opened: "There was tetrachlorodibenzodioxin which was teratogenic and mutagenic but the Town of Toxytort passed the anti-pollution ordinance before the County of Bigdump passed Resolution Eight. Mrs. Redacne signed the purchase money mortgage the year before and furthermore also. . . ."

Some lawyers are so full of knowledge that they've lost sight of the issues. Either we control knowledge or it controls us. The consummate lawyer's skill is to orient knowledge toward issues. It's tempting to accumulate knowledge without thinking about it. It's hard work to orient knowledge to issues.

Yet knowledge without purpose is a prescription for disaster.

Contrast Mr. Point with Mr. Stuffed. Point, too, has consulted with many experts and has much knowledge, but he always deals with issues.

> **Q.** *"When the fuel lines clog the engine will fail?"*
> **A.** *"Yes."*
>
> **Q.** *"The engine will fail because it will be starved for fuel?"*
> **A.** *"Yes."*

Knowledge with purpose is a prescription for success.

10. *Whosoever Exalts Himself Shall Be Humbled.* Some with great knowledge fail because they are proud. They like to show off.

Mr. Vanity: "Isn't it a fact that a rhabdomyosarcoma may be either pleomorphic or . . . ?" Oh, no! Mr. Vanity is the boy in class who always raised his hand when the one called on didn't know the answer. The other "kids" hated him then and the jurors don't like him much better.

Contrast Ms. Meek: "I'm not a chemist. I may mispronounce a few words. Please bear with me." Or "Excuse me, I don't look forward to asking you questions in your field, sir."

Most people prefer Ms. Meek.

MORAL: *Pride goeth before a fall.*

11. *Would That Mine Enemy Would Write a Book.* My favorite enemy expert is one who writes a lot. This is the age of the computer and the photocopier. Everybody is publishing or perishing. Even the dullest of souls are turning out articles, columns, pamphlets and books. Get it all. No one can be perpetually consistent. You'll find something. Maybe you'll even get somebody to admit à la Pegler (Westbrook Pegler sued by Quentin Reynolds for libel) that he doesn't agree with his own articles.

On the other hand, lawyers shouldn't write too much. This is the age of discovery. Assume everything you write to your expert and everything your expert writes to you will be seen by the other side. Therefore, don't write a letter saying you hope she'll find the cancer was caused by exposure to the defendant's product. You can already hear the other lawyer on cross: "You were told what to find, weren't you?"

Above all, don't show your expert confidential material.

Famous scenario: Once upon a time a trial lawyer in a large litigation showed his expert his trial book. A Magistrate ordered the book to be given to the other side. Disaster was averted by the Trial Judge, who reversed the order because the lawyer's entire trial strategy was in that book.

Anything brought to the stand may be seen. The adroit cross-examiner will almost always start by asking for the expert's file. It's amazing what you pick up that way. Doodlings showing doubts about calculations; prior complaints about the product. Some experts seem to have a death wish.

Old adage: Experts should bring nothing to the stand but their laundry tickets.

12. *There Is a Season for All Things.* Most experts are put on the stand either late or last. They serve as a summation. They put it all together. It is often effective.

But little should ever be done by rote or rule. Sometimes an expert can be your first witness. "What is the history of the power press?" "In the early 1900s, what guards were used?" "What standards of safety were there in the 1920s?" An awareness that for many decades the industry knew of the perils of the power press has been unquestionably established early in the trial. You have made your issue dominant.

The lawyer who selects the issues often wins the case.

13. *The Lowest Form of Argument Is the Ad Hominem Attack and Jurors Love It.* You can't dent Dr. Simon Smooth.

He knows more about orthopedic surgery than any ten bone doctors in the world. Simon Smooth deftly deflects all questions. He testifies twice weekly. He'll say anything for money—that is, lots of money. What do you do? Sink to the ad hominem. It's time to besmirch Simon Smooth.

> **Q.** *"How much are you charging?"*
>
> **A.** *"It depends on how long I'll be here."*
>
> **Q.** *"Suppose we were to stop now?"*
>
> **A.** *"I haven't added it up yet."*
>
> **Q.** *"Do it now. Please take your time."* Let him twist in the wind.

Lawyers love collateral cross. It's easy. You don't have to know what the expert knows. You just have to know a little about human nature and the root of all evil.

Needless to say, ad hominem isn't always appropriate. Buck Bull-horn, a former prosecutor, tears every witness to tatters. He has no mercy, no compunction and indeed no brains. Recently, he cross-examined an expert on theology, "And how much are you being paid to testify, Reverend?"

14. *The World Loves a Teacher.* There's something about teachers. We trust them. We remember kindly Miss Witherspoon from the first grade. We still believe every word she said. But we don't trust witnesses who are paid to testify. *Ergo:* Make your expert a teacher.

Ask basic questions. Ask for definitions. "What is a cranial nerve?" "What is a nerve?" "How does the eye move?"

And above all, get the expert off the stand and down to the jury. When the doctor stands near the jurors, they start to see her as a person. Let the expert use a blackboard or a visual aid that justifies her leaving the stand. Let her act as if she's in the operating room or the classroom, not the courtroom. Let her teach all those facts not in dispute about the nervous system. The jurors will start to believe her. Then, when the doctor gets to the only issue in the case, that is, whether the accident caused the paralysis, they are ready to believe her, she who has been their friendly teacher.

15. *One Picture Is Worth a Thousand Words.* The eye sees more than the ear hears. This is the age of television. We should not be just "word" lawyers.

Use a model for your architect to show the construction of a building. Use a chart for your economist to depict the impact of inflation. Use photographs, including blowups, so your engineer can show how the machine works. Let your automotive engineer describe the operation of the automobile engine that you brought into the courtroom, or your aeronautical engineer disassemble the model of the airplane engine. Let the photographer describe the contour of the road on the aerial photo. Let your physician use the blowups of the drawing from the medical textbook showing the ankle joint. Let your toxicologist use the graph prepared by a forensic artist just for your case to explain the toxicity of various chemicals.

Caveat A: Visual evidence must be fair and accurate. I've seen a Court refuse to admit a model of a fire scene which cost many thousands of dollars. There were too many deviations from the original. Worse yet, I've seen a trial lawyer use an elaborate model of a building that unfairly emphasized his contentions. The opponent—who didn't object to its introduction—excoriated the model for its blatant partiality. The jury agreed and the user of the model lost.

Caveat B: Beware of gimmicks. Anything "tricky" is to be avoided like the plague. Mr. Stagey just doesn't have a simple chart. He has a technicolor extravaganza in 3-D with assistants using pointers, all choreographed by the impresario Stagey. It's a great show. The only problem is that the jury knows it's being manipulated.

Contrast Mr. Stagey with a very natural trial lawyer who once talked of two cars. He used no fancy models. He took two sugar cubes from his pocket and described the crash. It was effective and unforced.

THE LESSON: Make your visual aid scrupulously fair and as untheatrical as possible.

16. *Practice Makes Perfect.* Ms. Impulse believes trial lawyers should be spontaneous. One day she surprised her fire expert, Smokey Burns, by asking him to show the jury how quickly the plastic ignites. Smokey Burns, who had just testified the plastic ignites instantly in the slightest presence of warmth, turned pale. He put a lit match to the plastic. Nothing happened. Burns lit another match. Nothing happened. The jury leaned forward. Burns turned red. He tried a third time. Nothing happened. Burns turned crimson. Burns tried again and again until he got a slight flicker. Ms. Impulse obliviously and triumphantly exclaimed, "For the record, may I state it's burning?" The Judge: "For the record, you may state it flickered."

Impulse violated cardinal rule "ninety-nine." Never, but never, do a demonstration in the courtroom unless you have performed it without mishap in your office ninety-nine times. *Caveat:* Whatever can go wrong will go wrong.

17. *All That Glitters Is Not Gold.* Dr. Yale Fakir boasts of magnificent credentials. He tells of his studies at the London Royal Academy of Surgeons, and how he recently lectured at the Istanbul conference giving a speech called "Supersurgery for Supersurgeons." Fred Squint glares at Dr. Fakir whom he's to cross-examine. Fred doesn't trust anybody. He says, "Everybody puffs a little." At recess, Fred starts to dig. Guess what? Fakir never went to the Royal Academy. He wasn't even invited to Istanbul. Dr. Fakir is a faker. The cross-examination is a trial lawyer's dream come true spiced with shouts of "fraud" and "to the District Attorney."

Most experts tell the truth about themselves. But crafty old trial lawyers teach us to be suspicious. They think the worst of people. And, sad to relate, they are often right.

18. *Enemy Experts Should Be Seen and Not Heard.* Ms. Innocent asks the enemy expert, Peter Blather, "Why?" You ask him—he'll tell you. It may take two or three hours and you'll feel like you've been run over by a steamroller, but he'll tell you. Blather loves to talk. He's paid to talk. It's his business. Don't give experts a chance to make speeches.

Adroit cross-examiners ask only "pin down" questions.

> **Good:** "Does the hospital chart say 'cyanosis'?"

> **Not as good:** "What is the significance of 'cyanosis'?"

> **Bad:** "Why do you say the patient had 'cyanosis'?"

Experts like Blather try to wiggle out of the pin-down leading questions asked by able questioners. "I can't answer that 'yes' or 'no,' I have to explain," repeats Blather over and over like a broken record. The lawyer says, "Your Honor, please make him answer 'yes' or 'no.'" The lawyer wants control. The expert wants freedom. An eternal tug of war.

19. *Testimony by Unpaid, Unsworn Experts Is Called "A Learned Treatise."* I love learned treatises. You read the great books. It costs nothing. You don't even have to take anybody to dinner. The jury knows the book wasn't written for your case. It makes for great comment in summation.

And they're even more fun on cross:

> "Doctor, don't you agree blood is red?"

> Trot out your ten books. Cite the page. Read pointedly and with meaningful looks.

> "Do you agree with Dr. Hematology that blood is red?"

> "With Hippocrates?"

> "Pasteur?"

Keep going and enjoy the expert who won't admit basic truths.

In some jurisdictions, the expert can try to frustrate the cross-examiner by refusing to concede the treatise is authoritative. That's even better.

Trot out the same ten books and the same meaningful looks.

"You don't admit that Einstein is an expert on the theory of relativity?"

"Did you know that Professor Gallen is Chair of the Department of Solar System Medicine at the Harvard— Yale—Johns Hopkins—Mayo Clinic? You don't admit he's an authority?"

"You admit you have Professor Galileo's book in your library? Isn't he an authority?"

"You admit you were taught by Isaac Newton at Princeton and you still deny he's an authority?"

"You say you are the only authority in your field?" "I rest."

Suggested antidote when the learned treatise ploy is pulled on you: Advise your experts to admit fairly what they truly believe is authoritative. Don't play games. The jury will see through a weasel who admits nothing.

In any event, a book is no problem. It's easy to distinguish a general statement in a text when it's truly not applicable. The expert uses the "but not in this case" counterploy. "Of course, fusion is an accepted surgical technique but not in the case of Mrs. Spineless."

SUGGESTION: When opposing counsel finishes a cross-examination with a learned treatise, ask with all innocence in front of the jury, "May I please see the book?" It's a very rare book when the next paragraph doesn't say, "On the other hand. . . ." And if you can use the enemy's book to make your point, you're halfway home. And sometimes a simple request to see the book disconcerts your opponent. One startled advocate stammered, "But it's my book. . . ." The jury no longer considered this paragon a seeker of truth and justice.

20. *The Trial Is a Game of Chess: Eighteen Little Gambits.*

I. *Set the Stage in Jury Selection.* The enemy expert, Dr. Glyn Glib, is a dangerous, effective witness. Rub a little gloss off her when questioning prospective jurors. "Have you ever sat on any case where Dr. Glib testified?" "Are you sure?"

II. *Don't Set the Stage.* If Glib is for you, be quiet. Let her arrive as an unsullied angel of truth.

III. *Jury Selection Is a Good Time to Introduce Dr. Sigmund Freud.* Your expert is Dr. Sigmund Freud. Mary has, he says, a traumatic neurosis, but the defense says she has a litigation neurosis. You had better explore prejudice now. "Would you judge the testimony of a psychiatrist the same as any other expert?" If Mr. Truckdriver is glaring at you with a look that says, "I've never heard of a neurosis that hard work wouldn't cure," you might remember that's why they gave us peremptory challenges.

IV. *Set the Stage in Opening.* Mention Dr. Glib again. "We'll prove she has testified in this kind of case for this lawyer at least five times." Otherwise, your first chance to show she's not St. Joan will be on cross. That may be psychologically too late after her impressive direct.

V. *Silence Is Golden.* Best not mention your expert's name during opening. You may have to use the spare instead. You call your expert Dr. Fickle the night before he's to testify. "What do you mean you've changed your mind that blood isn't always red?" Oh grave, where are you? Just describe "what" will be said, not "who" will say it.

VI. *Linger Over Great Qualifications.* Your expert is highly qualified. Take your time. You can only do well on this issue. *Danger:* The expert may look immodest. Therefore, let the expert be reticent and you pull it out step by step. "I don't mean to impose on your modesty, but please tell us. . . ."

Jurors love modest experts. They're a very rare species—almost extinct—but when you find one, rejoice at this curiosity of nature.

VII. *Gloss Over the Duds.* Your expert is not highly qualified. Use the hurry-up gambit. "I don't want to take the Court's time." "Let's get right to the case." Of course, if your opponent takes leave of her senses and concedes that Dr. Backbreaker is a qualified chiropractor, accept it with tears of gratitude.

VIII. *Act Like a Sweetheart, Think Like a Fox and Hope for Judge Oblivious.* Why not generously concede the qualifications of an eminently qualified expert? You don't want the jury to hear those magnificent credentials anyway and you might look gracious. Nobody in his right mind will accept the concession, right? Well, you never know. Occasionally, Judge Oblivious will grow impatient with a lawyer refusing a concession. "Counsel, you can't do better than a concession." And some poor weak-willed lawyer might capitulate and accept it.

IX. *Use the Sidebar Gambit.* The expert has pathetic qualifications. You feel you can disqualify him as a witness. Rather than "voir dire" in front of the jury, throw out a nonchalant "May we approach, Your Honor?" This usually gets an affirmative nod. At the sidebar: "Judge, this guy shouldn't testify. I want a full cross on his qualifications in the absence of the jury. It's a question of law." You may succeed in disqualifying the witness or you may not. In either event, you don't want to appear obstructive to the jury. They usually don't like objections. They want to hear it all. That's why we sometimes discreetly use the sidebar gambit.

X. *Why Not Sum Up Twice?* In many jurisdictions, the hypothetical may be shortened and not all the supporting facts need be recited. But occasionally we like to use the full hypothetical as a summation.

Assume Joseph Worker's arm was caught and torn off in the compactor made by the Heartless Company. Assume the compactor had no cutoff switch. Assume further that at the time Joe's arm was amputated there was no warning whatsoever on the compactor. Assume there was no guard preventing an arm from entering the compactor. Also assume that the safety engineer for the Heartless Company recommended that a cutoff switch and a guard be placed on the compactor before it was designed. Assume that before this compactor was made three reports of accidents with identical compactors involving amputated arms were given to the Heartless Company. Assume . . . assume . . . do you have an opinion . . .? Why not?

XI. *Be a Matador.* Cross-examining an expert is like bullfighting. The bull is dangerous. Do it fast. If you don't kill him, he may kill you.

XII. *Tell Diogenes We Found One.* Honest Abe is their expert. His credentials are impeccable. His assumptions are supported. His conclusions are reasonable. We have another rare one: the totally honest expert.

How do we cross? SUGGESTION: Paint your picture! Whatever can be proven through the enemy's mouth will be believed.

> "Was John gasping when admitted to the hospital?" "Was he turning blue?" "Does turning blue show a lack of oxygen?" "Does the brain need oxygen?" "If deprived of oxygen, will the brain die?" "Is John now brain-damaged and retarded?"

Pile "yes" upon "yes" like a mason building a foundation.

XIII. *Even Babe Ruth Couldn't Play Every Position.* Their expert is overextended. They're using him for everything. Dr. Everytopic testifies that the insecticide is not dangerous, that Joe has emphysema from smoking and that Bill has heart disease due only to heredity.

This is a delicious opportunity. Dr. Everytopic can't know everything.

"Did you know Joe stopped smoking four years ago?"

"Did you know Bill's cholesterol went to 330 after he started the job?

"How old was Bill's father when he died?"

Just keep going with the "Did you know?" kind of cross. It's easy and the legal equivalent of torture.

XIV. *Use the "No Recess" Gambit.* The cross is going well. The rhythm is yours. The judge asks, "Is this a good time to break?" You: "I'd appreciate just a few moments to finish this line." After halftime, Mr. Expert may come back corrected; his coaches may have spotted ways to help him. And even when the other side is not allowed to talk to him, the rhythm may be lost after recess. Finish him off now. You're on a roll.

XV. *Use the Recess Gambit.* Your brilliant know-it-all expert is being shredded beyond recognition on cross. "Your Honor, may we have a few moments, please? A matter of personal necessity, sir. Thank you."

XVI. *Tell It Like It Is.* Sometimes you have to let it rip. The jury knows some experts are nothing more than hessians. When one of these partisans goes over the line, don't mince words.

> SUMMATION: "Mr. Honest is an honorable man. He was honorable the last thirty times he testified and never found anything wrong and always for 200 pieces of silver an hour. . . ."

XVII. *Don't Forget the Charge.* Nobody has to believe an expert and the judge will tell that to the jury.

XVIII. *Brevity Is the Soul of Wit, or Direct Revisited.* Mr. Long-winded starts Professor Ramble through his direct. Four days later they finish. It is a masterful exercise leaving nothing to the imagination. The trial has lasted four months and the judge was understandably indulgent about the exorbitant length of the direct. Some cases need this full dissertation with all points covered. But I wonder.

Mr. Quick starts Professor Crystal through his direct. Thirty minutes later they finish. The trial has lasted four months. The courtroom is agog since Professor Crystal was the main expert. Has Mr. Quick lost his senses? I think not.

When in doubt, be brief. It takes much effort to be brief. Old gag: "I didn't have the time to write a short letter."

Compression is a lawyer's art. Marvelous are those advocates who with a lifetime of practice can condense a rambling narrative into a short, clear statement, encapsulating the essence in but a few words.

The direct of the major expert can be a distillation of your case. Get to the heart. Find the crucial issue that divides the parties. No jury will resolve the million quibbles in a warehouse of documents. Most cases are ultimately decided on one or two basic propositions. Jurors are searching for the jugular of the case.

Obtain from your expert those brief answers which, if believed, win the case. Leave the petty quibbles to cross. Give the cross-examiner a small target. The jury will remember your direct. It was all muscle and sinew. With audacity, you have built your case and hurled the challenge: tear it down if you can.

This then is the lawyer's art: to take a multitude of facts and contentions strung across countless years of litigation and compress them into a gem of crystal clarity. While not easy, it is a stunning opportunity and greatly rewarding.

In living with experts, not only do we want to survive, we want to prevail.

NINE SECRETS FOR LIVING WITH JUDGES

"A judge is a law student who marks his own examination paper."

—H. L. Mencken

"The thing to fear is not the law but the judge."

—Russian proverb

T HE LEGENDARY AUSTRALIAN BARRISTER ADDISON STEELE recently regaled visiting American lawyers on the vagaries of judges from the Land Down Under. Addison described the secrets employed by the Australian bar in its dealings with the bench. He named names. His lecture displayed rare candor and deserves repeating in America:

1. *Enlighten Judge Dimness.* Marlowe Dimness descends from a prominent family long renowned in the political life of New South Wales. Unfortunately, before ascending the bench, Judge Dimness never entertained a passion for the practice of law. He neither knows the law nor has a quick grasp of it. However, he possesses other attributes of high quality—scrupulous honesty and unfailing courtesy. Jurors love him, and lawyers wish him well.

But Judge Dimness exasperates Carl Cocky, a lawyer who deeply admires his own brilliance. Cocky throws his attaché case on the counsel table in disgust, raises his eyes in exasperation at the dumbness of Dimness. Cocky doesn't submit briefs on difficult points, thinking them beyond Dimness's capacity. Cocky attacks Dimness whenever he can. Jurors, who don't know Dimness is dim, resent Cocky, and appellate courts don't appreciate Cocky. That's how not to do it.

Lawyer Kate Kean submits briefs on all major points. With modesty, she discusses issues with the judge's legal assistant. She knows Dimness often looks to his legal assistant, who nods yes or no for rulings. She never lets on she knows Dimness is dim. Subtly, sincerely, she tries to educate him. She never shows him up. When Dimness errs, she fully but politely protects the record. She never attacks him. She fortifies him. She even praises him: "With the greatest respect, no, I mean it, I do respect your desire to reach the right result." She doesn't belittle him. She tries to enlighten Judge Dimness and more often than not brings out the best in him. She tries to help him. That's how to do it.

However, Marlowe Dimness has a cousin, the Honorable Malcolm Dimness, who descends from a prominent family long renowned in the political life of Victoria. Malcolm is as dim as Marlowe but not nearly as sweet. Malcolm is arrogant. Unfortunately, ignorance and arrogance often keep company. Judge Malcolm covers up by bullying. He yells at lawyers: "Stand up!" "Sit down!" "Stay at the lectern!" "Don't talk!" He constantly tells the jury of his great burden in dealing with unprepared and unintelligent lawyers.

Kate treats Malcolm the same as Marlowe, only more so. She exudes even more respect. She smiles with even more deference as she submits basic briefs on basic points. She also looks in the mirror every day of the trial and prays: "Lord, give me the patience to smile at Malcolm Dimness! Give me the courage to endure the human comedy!"

2. *Anticipate Judge Swift.* Judge Swift is fast, very fast. He makes his mind up quickly. Paul Ponderous speaks slowly, comes laboriously to the point, and does very poorly before Judge Swift. As Ponderous warms up, Swift decides.

While Ponderous stumbles, Sidney Smart sprints. For Judge Swift, he takes extra pains to prepare. He anticipates all issues by having ready two or three sentences, succinct sentences, to answer Swift's specific questions. As quickly as Swift asks, Smart replies.

He knows that appearing before Swift can make him a better lawyer by forcing him to get right down to business.

Sometimes Swift tries to hurry even the fast-moving Smart. Smart resists the steamroller: "Your Honor, I appreciate the concession, but it is essential that you hear my expert's qualifications."

Other times Swift is so fast he makes his mind up before the case begins. Smart appeals to the very intelligent but too confident Swift, "I ask for the gift of an open mind, Your Honor, you haven't heard it all." Swift may listen; he doesn't like to be wrong.

3. *Stiffen Judge Lax.* Judge Wadsworth Lax enjoys the affection of the bar in Hobart, capital of the island state of Tasmania. He smiles even in the face of provocation. He seeks a fair resolution of all disputes. He has a scholar's knowledge. He has one drawback: He never restrains counsel. He doesn't like to offend anyone. Pandemonium replaces decorum in his courtroom. Lawyers fight like Tasmanian devils in his presence.

Quincy Quarrelsome loves to appear before Judge Lax. Nasty by nature, he loves to fight with his opponent. He objects with long improper speeches. Adversaries appealing to Judge Lax for help receive bromides like "Now, counsel, you both know better."

Alfred Swagman takes no guff from anyone, least of all Quincy. First, he appeals to Judge Lax's pride without embarrassing him. He knows the refusal to discipline counsel flows from the judge's insecurity. He diplomatically points out the loss of respect for the judicial process that chaos in the courtroom produces: "Judge Lax, what must the jurors think of this constant fighting? It detracts from your dignity. Your Honor, please restrict counsel, both of us, to objections without arguments. Forbid personal insult and cross talk between counsel. Insist we address the court only in argument. I ask you to reprimand whoever violates your directions." Inwardly, Judge Lax knows Swagman is right. Sometimes one can stiffen Judge Lax. But sometimes one cannot. If all else fails, Swagman must answer Quarrelsome, relying on experience and praying for wit. If Swagman acts like the "good guy," a long trial, especially, will usually expose Quarrelsome as the "bad guy" who—jurors may sense—disrespects the judge, the system, the world, and, indeed, everyone in it.

4. *Excite Judge Listless.* Robert William Listless never wanted to be a judge. He adores rugby. He knows the name of every player in the rugby league in Sydney and Brisbane. He waxes eloquent over the intricacies of a scrummage. Sometimes he leaves court early to watch his favorite team practice. During his rather lengthy luncheons and midday recesses, Listless shows an excitement in discussing rugby rarely displayed when he talks law. Secretly, he never enjoyed the law. His father and wife wouldn't hear of his desire to make a career of coaching a rugby team. Law is more respectable, they argued. Listless became a judge, but he doesn't like it. He never takes work home. He can hardly wait to leave the courthouse. John Oak has an important cause with many witnesses and scheduling problems, a cause teeming with complicated legal issues, a cause in need of prompt resolution. John has been assigned for trial to Judge Listless. What can John do? Somehow he must excite Judge Listless. But how? First, appeal to his sense of justice: "Might we work a bit beyond four o'clock today, Your Honor? Professor Geldbeutel must return to Vienna tonight." Or, "Could we take a shorter lunch break this week, Judge, to help complete the trial, since my client will be fired if she misses work next week?" Or, "Your Honor, would you conclude this hearing on custody before your vacation, since I fear for the child's safety?" Or try appealing to his vanity: "Your Honor, no one has been able to settle this dispute. I believe you can do it." Do it humbly: "I need your help, Your Honor. Here is the problem." Keep trying. Don't give up. If all else fails, you can always plead, beg, or kneel. You might even try crying. The secret of Judge Listless is that beneath his indifference are remnants of decency. Pierce that shell to break through to his dormant better self. Lazy people have often never known the joy of deep involvement and hard work. Listless protects himself by trying not to get involved. Overcome his indifference. Show him the picture of the horribly maimed little girl. Ignite those embers not yet entirely extinguished even in a Judge Listless.

5. *Challenge Judge Slant.* With a squint of his eyes, the Honorable Richard Hawke Slant furtively recognizes friends in the courtroom. After many years in many clubhouses, the politically aware Slant enjoys many friends, and they enjoy him. Slant stares down lawyers who are strangers, particularly when they are young and easily intimidated. It surprises Slant in a vaguely unpleasant way that women now appear before him. Although Slant favors friends, he presides carefully, ever mindful of the record. Nettie Wickersham, a young advocate, starts by giving Judge Slant the benefit of the doubt. She has no chip on her shoulder that might invite a knock. In the privacy of his chambers, she gently suggests, "Your Honor, I know it was unintended, but you frowned when I asked the last question." If Slant persists, Nettie does not shrink. She protects the record: "Your Honor, I respectfully object to the tone of your voice when you disallowed my objection, and to your smiling at my opponent when he addresses you." Nettie asserts herself, hoping the jurors will sense the bias—which may boomerang against the malevolent Slant. Jurors generally favor judges. However, once on your side, the jury will support a lawyer all the way against a prejudiced judge. Some lawyers go so far as to encourage the bias of a Slant to make it even more obvious. Nettie, mannerly but fearlessly vocal when she needs to be, has already earned the respect of bench and bar. She presumes the fairness of all judges but rises to challenge when Judge Slant leans.

6. *Love Judge Grumpseat.* Judge Edward Fitzhugh Grumpseat looks coldly at all humanity. Some disappointment, inflicted on him while young, haunts his every gesture and unsmiling face. Sometimes he smiles, as when he boasts "I eat young lawyers for breakfast." Dyspeptic and disagreeable, he growls at everyone equally, irrespective of race, gender, or creed. When appearing before Grumpseat, alert the jurors during their selection that you may not always agree with the judge. "I certainly intend no disrespect, but it will be my duty to speak up on behalf of my client." You must prepare the jurors. Grumpseat awaits you. You may have to make a record. Appellate Judges know the Grumpseats of this world. You cannot be a wimp with Judge Grumpseat. But why not begin by trying to pacify him? Search for the young boy in him who always smiled before life turned him into a modern Scrooge. Love Judge Grumpseat. He knows everybody hates him. If nothing else, love will at least surprise and perhaps disconcert him. Kill him with kindness. At the least, the jury will be amazed at your patience on your client's behalf. Edge right up to unctuousness: "Your Honor, I am truly sorry I asked the question awkwardly. Give me a chance to reword it." Grumpseat may say "I'm sick and tired of your apologies." This may get a smile of approval for you from the jury. Or, Grumpseat may, despite himself, feel a stirring of his long buried humanity. Try loving Grumpseat. Why not? Understand him. To understand is to forgive. Rescue Grumpseat from himself. This might even make you a better person.

7. *Flatter Judge Prideface.* With great pride, Lord Henry Winthrop Prideface traces his ancestry back to one of the convicts who originally settled Australia. This brings great dignity to him—comparable to the dignity of American descendants of the Mayflower Pilgrims. Although he is short of stature, no one stands taller in a courtroom than Lord Prideface, a Judge often rumored as a candidate for the High Court of Australia itself. When Judge Prideface speaks, all listen. He demands and receives additional personnel to staff his courtroom. He is smart, knowledgeable, articulate, and intensely desirous of favorable publicity. He always courts favor among journalists. He has no doubt as to his prowess; he would invade Russia in the winter.

Lawyers should tell Judge Prideface of his greatness; he will believe them. But be careful: be keen of mind, for he will see through transparent fawning. Subtlety will do it. He desperately wants the flattery to be true. Try something like "Much obliged for your analysis, Judge. It showed me the way." Or, "I appreciate your control over the courtroom, Judge Prideface. This is the way cases should be tried. Sorry to say, not everyone measures up to your standard." Judge Prideface may not love you for these tributes because he believes them to be his absolute due. But, perhaps—and who can ask for anything more—he might not do you any harm. Still, though, you worry. You believe lawyers should offer only truthful praise. Agreed. But in Prideface's case, just tell the truth more emphatically. You still worry. Prideface, sharp of mind, may detect insincerity in your praise. Don't fret. Remember Dean Swift's words:

> 'Tis an old maxim in the schools,
> That flattery's the food of fools;
> Yet now and then your men of wit
> Will condescend to take a bit.

8. *Revere Judge Goode.* Francis Goode is a great jurist. The Melbourne Bar calls him "our good mate." Courageous, honorable, scholarly, he disarms people with a kindly understanding of human frailty. He settles more cases than anyone else in his courthouse. He never takes himself seriously, but lowers himself with a deprecating humor. He arises early, works late, and worries passionately over the cases assigned to him. He does not inject himself into the trial except to prevent an injustice by helping a stumbling advocate. He tolerates no lawyer's shouting colloquy or arguing objections. He runs a tight ship and is quick to discipline any mutinous barrister. But because the atmosphere is relaxed and friendly, he brings out the best in the advocates. Lawyers yearn to be assigned to him. Lawyers should thank Judge Goode. He is a gift. He is a trial lawyer's reward. Lawyers should aspire to his level. For Judge Goode, the advocate must be prepared, well prepared. Never try to fool him or any other Judge. Judge Goode comes close to perfection, and we should revere him, but perfection among humans is rare. Therefore, to be fair, we must. . . .

9. *Judge Judges Gently.* The percentage of inadequate lawyers probably exceeds the percentage of inadequate judges. For every Judge Dimness, there are ten Mr. Thicknesses too dense to see the issue even when they fall over it. For every Judge Slant, there are countless Percy Slitherses who have never yet had thoughts in their heads other than for calculating their fees. Judge Lax would never have a problem of discipline if it were not for the cave dwelling Rambo Bigmouths, who think of weakness as an opportunity to exploit. And Judge Prideface did not first become proud upon ascending the bench. He derives from that majority of humankind who crave power. They can be found everywhere: as clerks in bureaus, for instance, or officials in uniform.

You don't like Judge Listless? Then meet Nellie Proforma, a lawyer who does it by the book. She hasn't exerted her imagination in an age. It's easier to use a form book. You don't like Judge Grumpseat? What about Mr. Bull? Have you seen him at a deposition? He uses his horns to spear anyone who disagrees with him. No, please. Don't moan about the foibles of judges without first cataloging the infirmities of lawyers.

Judges today must endure inadequate counsel, crowded dockets, and public cynicism, as well as the spectacle of lawyers half their age earning twice as much as they do. Why do they take it?

At the turn of the century, judges rode the circuit in the lonely spaces of the Outback. A long-forgotten judge on horseback would arrive one day a month in a remote bush town to hold court in a one-room schoolhouse with windows tightly shut to keep out the windblown dust. An admiring lawyer, visiting from Sydney, nailed to the wooden wall this tribute:

> *Let us remember to honor the judges, for they are dedicated to the peaceful resolution of human disputes. We should not take civility or even civilization for granted.*

I have known many a jurist who, possessed of compassion as well as erudition, has labored long into the night to craft an opinion because time was essential to the litigants. I have known many who have taken a new case late in the day to aid a beleaguered colleague.

I have known many who treat all with courtesy, who help the defeated believe they had a fair day in court, and who with wisdom avoid defeat for all by bringing about a reasonable settlement. I have known many whose mind is always open to fair argument, whose pursuit of truth is not impeded by prejudice of any kind, whose integrity is unquestionable, whose good humor relaxes the bitterest of foes, whose goodness is contagious, and whose humility is unfailing. I have known many, and I speak to them now: when the sacrifices you make discourage you, remember that your commitment to justice and the respect it earns can still produce the sweetest of rewards. At the end, we will measure our lives, not by the wealth we have garnered, but by the goodness we have done, the kindness we have bestowed, and the peace of mind we have achieved.

Chapter

9

LIVING
WITH DEFEAT

"It is defeat that makes men invincible."

—H. W. Beecher

"There are defeats more triumphant than victories."

—Montaigne

I TRY CASES FOR INJURED PLAINTIFFS. PLEASE DO NOT STOP reading. We may have much in common. I pick juries, open, examine, cross-examine, close, listen to charges, and, yes, I lose cases.

Trying cases is meat and drink, but losing cases is something else. Think of those sleepless nights filled with guilt and doubt. And there is never any rest; we face defeat in every single trial. It is enough to make you plan estates.

Many years ago, Jeremiah Sage, the famous trial lawyer, gave a speech the bluntness of which still lingers:

> *"Young lawyers think trying cases is all glory. But trial lawyers pay a price unknown to our armchair colleagues who never stray beyond the safety of their desks. Trial lawyers lose cases.*

> *Did you ever hear of a lawyer's losing a contract? If you lose a trial, every explanation seems lame. The client who adored yesterday's summation glares at you in disgust after today's defeat. The jury has rejected you. It's a personal defeat. It burns in memory. Defeat is the price trial lawyers pay for success."*

Sage was caustic but wise. Trying cases is easy if you can live with defeat. But some cannot stand it.

Consider these profiles in defeat.

Howard Fear tries a good case. He can cross-examine with the best. He has a busy practice. Yet he has not taken a verdict in five years. He has as many excuses as cases. The judge was weak; the jury was weak; the witness was weak; the case was weak. In truth, it is Mr. Fear who is weak. When he is a plaintiff, any offer will settle. When he is a defendant, he terrifies clients into settlement. He has lost his zest for combat.

Howard still broods over his humiliating loss years ago to George Gloat. Every time Howard meets George they shake hands politely, but Howard can neither forgive nor forget. It eats at him.

Worse, Howard's colleagues know he will not take a verdict. They drive hard bargains. Howard knows they know. The courthouse joke: what rhymes with Howard? Howard will retire early. Being a trial lawyer is no longer fun.

Erasmus Nasty has just lost a case. He, who believes he can control every mood in the courtroom, has just lost a case. Erasmus is polite to the judge and the jury. But in his office, Erasmus is his true self. The staff braces for the attack. Secretaries cringe. Young associates cower. Invariably, following defeat, Erasmus will fire his investigator for incompetence. Heads will roll and invective will flow. Erasmus will hibernate in his office. It will be months before he emerges. Erasmus is irascible and nasty.

P. J. Broods cannot get over a loss. She broods and sulks and relives every question. She cares about her client; she is not afraid to take a verdict; she has not lost her civility. She just has no spirit. She sits quietly in her office with the lights lowered. Other cases seem unimportant; life seems meaningless. Her whole self is consumed in replaying the trial. She dwells on it. She cannot find it in her character to put it behind her. P. J. Broods cannot put it in perspective.

And then there is J. P. Lukewarm. Lukewarm loses a lot of cases, but never his smile. "Nothing is worth an ulcer," sighs Lukewarm. He compares himself to a painter. "Each trial is my painting. If the jurors don't like it, it's not my problem." He protects himself by the oldest of devices: he does not care. He will not risk the pain of defeat. Lukewarm never permits passion, never takes a chance. He is an empty pleader. Jurors just do not believe Lukewarm. He brings no conviction to his causes. To the local trial bar, Lukewarm is known as the "Smiling Punching Bag." He is a loser.

Leo Fury is different. He is mean. He is mean even when he wins. They call him "Leo, the Sore Winner." Leo always expects to win. Once, before a verdict, he planned a party to celebrate victory and had his tuxedo laid out in advance. He denies it is hubris; he calls it intelligent confidence.

Even the judges give Leo wide berth in defeat. His fury knows no bounds. After an adverse verdict he once harangued a court for two hours in the guise of a motion. Lawyers, wide-eyed in amazement, came to listen as Leo castigated and denounced. Across from the courthouse, in the Alibi Tavern, Leo made his darkest allegations about the corruption of witnesses. "This case will never be over," sputtered Leo, as he personally served the Notice of Appeal. Leo was angry—angry with the judge for stupidity, the witnesses for cupidity, and his opponent for just being an opponent. Leo was furious at everyone except himself. Leo can never lose. He measures himself by his victories. A defeat therefore diminishes him. He is all vanity. He is absurd.

The last and most mysterious profile is Rex Stunningham's. Rex has it all. First a prosecutor and now a private practitioner, Rex is among the very best advocates in the country. Always polite, invariably candid, unquestionably ethical, and unhesitatingly generous in representing the needy without fee or in lecturing to young lawyers, he is the very model of the best in our profession. His handsome face and pleasing personality have made him a darling of the media. Rex is well known to the general public.

Some years ago, John Plain, a vigorous, no-nonsense trial lawyer, beat Rex, fair and square. Rex took it badly. Rex has not talked to John since the verdict. John Plain, a good man, met Rex recently, held out his hand, smiled and said, "How's my old friend?" Rex refused his hand and walked away. Curious.

Were we to have seen Rex alone in the privacy of his den on the night of the defeat, it would have been even more curious. Face flushed with drink and eyes moist with bitter tears, he would have been heard to mutter, "That I should lose to John Plain, a nobody." Very curious.

Can we unravel this mystery? What is the failing common to Rex and each of these flawed lawyers? I believe it is pride. These advocates think they alone make the difference between victory and defeat. Some of them strut mightily across courtrooms as if they were monarchs of all they survey. They are preposterous. They are tiny specks. The universe is indifferent to their very existence.

Advocates must love combat. Without competitiveness, they cannot function. But pride is the sin that goeth before a fall. It is the client's case, not ours. We should know our place.

And sometimes we should lose. Defeat may be a just result, although it may take us some years to realize it.

Some lawyers know how to live with defeat. Jeremiah Sage tried a case against Tom Young, honorable but inexperienced. Jeremiah, at the peak of his fame, was expected to win. He lost. It had been a long time since Jeremiah lost. Following the verdict, the jury was polled and excused; motions were resolved; the judge left; the courtroom was quiet. Jeremiah rose and approached his opponent. "Tom, you tried a fine case." Jeremiah shook his hand, left the courtroom, and returned the next day as awesome as ever.

Jeremiah had a ritual by which he exorcised defeat. He knew he had to mount the horse again. He approached a new trial with vigor, determined to show he was ready to take a verdict. He knew his adversaries would be studying his every move to see if he was shy of combat. Jeremiah almost preferred to take a verdict following a loss rather than settle. Yet he put client before self in making that decision.

But not everybody is a Jeremiah. The crosscurrents of the advocate's mind following defeat are subtle. "Take a verdict or they'll think you're afraid if you settle. But it's a good offer and I should take it because my client comes first. But in the office they say it's a great case and I shouldn't settle. But I'd better settle because I can't afford to lose two or three in a row or I'll be back on the pleadings desk."

Dear lawyers, we all tend to exalt the fiction of our great reputations. In truth, most of our defeats do not make page one. Most times our peers couldn't care less, except for the momentary pleasure the perverse will always take at a colleague's setback. Better to emulate Jeremiah. Get up. Resume the race. And stop worrying about ourselves.

How does Jeremiah do it? He puts things in perspective. Listen to him:

> "I lost a case as a young lawyer and thought the world would come to an end. But it didn't. I didn't go to jail. I wasn't disbarred. I went home. My family was still there. There was food on the table. And the next morning, most amazing of all, the sun did rise and a new day began."

Mr. Sage puts things in perspective. He has philosophy.

How can one achieve philosophy? Ironically, defeat helps. Adversity's sweet milk may indeed be philosophy. The only trial lawyers who do not lose cases are those who do not try cases, who settle too many cases, or who take only cases that are such sure winners they do not need a trial lawyer to try them. Defeat is inevitable for the active litigator. It just takes a little time to get used to it. Defeat, after all, is an acquired taste.

We must accept that in our careers we are going to lose a certain number of cases. We just do not know which ones they will be. We must either accept that or become a distorted half-person like Mr. Fear or Mr. Fury. We should remember that a lawyer will not be judged by one case. Anybody can win or lose a big case. It is the pattern of a career that establishes superior advocacy.

There is, however, an inexcusable defeat. We did not prepare; we did not make the effort; we did not do all we should have done. I do not refer to mere errors of judgment. We all choose the wrong juror, ask a dumb question, fail to object, or object when we should not. Hopefully, these are the mistakes from which we will learn.

By the inexcusable, I refer to that laziness for which there is no defense. We did not prepare a crucial witness personally but left it to an aide. We fumbled during the cross-examination of the expert because we did not take time to index the previous testimony. We did not spend enough time preparing our summation even though we had the weekend. We did not go to the scene, and so we lacked authenticity in describing it. We should be sleepless. We should have long nights. We are guilty.

The courtroom seems to me to be a small mirror of the larger world. The unbearable troubles are those we bring on ourselves.

Putting defeat in perspective may be the secret of great trial lawyers. Having conquered the dread of defeat, they are even more formidable. Adversaries see in their eyes a willingness to take verdicts. Jurors do not find their confidence betrayed by nervousness. Free of fear, these advocates cannot wait to try cases. The joy of battle has not been leaked away in needless worry. These advocates can try cases to the last day they live, while others retire early to play golf or write articles about advocacy.

Then let defeat come. While we will not welcome it, we will not fear it. Take it by the neck, shake it, subdue it, put it in its place. All it takes is character—the advocate's highest attribute.

Victory is no challenge. In defeat, advocates discover their character. Only in affliction did Job discover his fortitude.

Paradoxes abound. Philosophers accept death and become wiser. Great trial lawyers accept defeat and become stronger.

In seeking to perfect the manners and morals of advocates, can we agree that the ultimate source of strength is that largeness of spirit which permits the gracious acceptance of defeat?

Chapter

10

COURAGE, OR TRYING A CASE WHEN THE JUDGE AND JURY HATE YOU

"The timorous may stay home."

—Benjamin N. Cardozo

"If we but face our difficulties, they will fly before us."

—Joseph Story

What they never told us in law school about a trial lawyer was the need for courage. A good voice, a clear mind, a capacity to reduce complexity, an ability to discover and select issues, a winning manner, a quickness under pressure, studiousness, knowledge, endurance, a massive will to win—all of these were cited as the necessary qualities of the advocate. Yet, no one mentioned bravery.

The necessity for courage remains a secret among the practitioners of that arcane art known as trial lawyering. Perhaps the point can be illustrated by a series of vignettes from different cases.

In any event, the hopefully practical purpose of these random remarks will be to help each of us get through the trial lawyer's day by sharing some common doubts and easing our isolation.

Down to the courthouse you go to select the jury of your dreams. You meet your peers in the corridor. You engage in the ancient ritual of testing each other.

"What kind of case you got?" Be careful that the case does not sound too weak. It will then be suspected that "business" is less than robust and questionable cases are being taken.

But suppose the case is made to sound promising. Then with a calculating and bottomless malevolence your brother at the bar smilingly will whisper to you, "Good luck, you've got a great case. There's no way you can lose." Oh, there is cruelty worthy of Caligula. Now if you lose the case there is but one explanation: you are an incompetent nincompoop.

You know your fellow trial lawyers will be immensely solicitous and then discreetly ask each other, "How did he ever lose that case?" You go into the jury room with your briefcase and fear.

JURY SELECTION

The mind of the advocate during jury selection is an unedited torrent of anxiety:

"She smiled at me—maybe it's a trap—she wants to sit—don't trust her—beware of hyphenated names—maybe she'll identify."

"She scowled at my adversary—she hates him—why not—so do I—he's unctuous—but she listens to his every word—look at the way she says she can vote for his case if the evidence supports it—what evidence—she hasn't heard anything yet."

> *"Her husband is an engineer—they wouldn't give anybody money unless a slide rule said so—she lives in Blunderstone—great plaintiff's country—she teaches English—she'll be judging me—but she'll like style."*
>
> *"Oh, she coaches the high school drama club—great!—she has feeling—I can reach out to her—human to human—she's for me— she is juror number three."*

With faith, hope and a tremulous heart, you say, "Jury satisfactory."

It happened during the testimony of the second witness. It was unmistakable. All the other jurors chuckled. Juror number three frowned when you put together a brilliant and rather droll bit of direct. She frowned. She turned her head.

What happened? She was attentive during opening. Who ever knows what happened? But it's no mistake, she hates you. What should you do? You can't settle the case because your opponent offers nothing. Just as well, you might be wrong and undersell. You can't surrender. That's just not done.

What can you do? You do what advocates have done since Darrow tried to save his neck. You fight back. You tighten your belt. You proceed. It's a long trial. Try to love her; maybe she'll love you back. If Daniel Webster could turn the jury of the damned around, maybe you can move juror number three.

It happened during the architect's testimony. Judge Despot told you to sit down. You know his reputation for short temper. You prepared the jury in selection by emphasizing that they alone can judge facts.

You are not a judge baiter. You, therefore, try by a soft word to turn away wrath. You can't. Old Judge Despot hates your case. He tells you unequivocally of his disdain at the next recess. You politely suggest in private that he may not have been as kindly and indulgent as he normally is. He is implacable. He belittles your case in front of the jury constantly.

You are now without choice. Emboldened by the inviolable rights of your client, you protest, always with genuine respect. You protect the record.

Where there is error, there must be exception. The jury might respect you more. Your opponent is uncomfortable and tries to stimulate the judge to belittle his own case.

The judge threatens you with contempt. You know you're respectful and that the judge is wrong. You don't want to be held in contempt. It means notoriety. There's no way you can win. Other judges will remember you. If there's a next time, you will already be marked. You are afraid. You are tempted to capitulate.

You look at your client. You find yourself. "Your Honor, with genuine respect, I protest your belittling of my client's cause and ask that the jury be instructed that they alone must decide the case." You found your heart. It's the least you could do. After all, old Malesherbes was rewarded with the guillotine for representing Louis XVI during the Reign of Terror.

THE COLLAPSE

You call Mary Lou to the stand. She is the pivotal witness. She collapses. She recants her story. She is so nervous under cross that she agrees with the cross-examiner that her narrative was a fiction inspired by you. In truth, you told her to tell the truth, but, by now the judge and the jury are glaring at you.

Your opponent suggests at a luncheon that this may be a case for the D.A. You see yourself in Alcatraz. Your life at the bar may become a memory. What do you do? You can't run away. You cannot go to Acapulco.

You have to stand up and conduct the redirect. "Didn't I tell you to tell the truth?" Objection. "Well, didn't I?" Objection. "Well, why didn't you say so?" Objection. You persevere. You struggle back up the hill part way. You create a doubt at least as to your villainy. The trial continues. Take heart and remember Dreyfus.

Your opponent, Mr. Crafty, cunning in the ways of human weakness, has deliberately made a tempting offer to settle. He offered you half of what you believe to be true settlement value. You know that your probability of success is high, but of course any case can be lost.

You have never been a glutton holding out for the last penny. You have never sought the headline of a successful verdict. You can afford to lose, but your client can't. Yet this offer is too low.

Your client says, "I think it's very low. But you're the lawyer, what do you think?" You think it's low but doubts beset you: If I lose, we get nothing. You never know what a jury will do. It would be very embarrassing to lose this case.

Your nerves reach out like tentacles to squeeze your spirit. Then you find yourself and resolutely reply, "I agree. It's low. Sure, we can lose, but the probabilities favor us." Tremulously but resolutely, you push forward, mindful of but trying to forget the spurned offer.

THE BIG MISTAKE

On your deathbed you will remember the calamity of your cross of Mrs. Callaghan. She was the prosecution's chief witness, and you had been destroying her. But then some inner devil made you violate centuries of lawyers' wisdom: you asked one more question. Mrs. Callaghan replied, "Because he told me he robbed three other banks."

The judge refuses to strike it. "You asked for it, counsellor!" The jurors elbow each other. Word spreads in the corridor. Your peers wear knowing smiles. Some pointedly turn not to see you; others turn pointedly to see you. Oh, how embarrassing!

You cry out to heaven, "Why didn't I become an actor? I'm going into Trusts and Estates. Oh, Death, where is thy sting!" The only salvation is humility. There is no other way of getting through the trial lawyer's day. Even the overweeningly proud and vain need a touch of it to survive.

Yet, after that question, what do you do? You laugh at yourself. Maybe you tell the jury, "I guess I shouldn't have asked that question." You continue. You recall the great trinity of qualities necessary to the survival of the daily practicing advocate: Wit, Humility and Courage, each of which supports the others.

SUMMATION

You now must sum up and the jury hates you. Juror number three glares at you as if you were a bug. She turns her head away as you rise to address the jury. You are disconcerted. You are tired and don't want to be tested today. Oh, but every day is a test day for trial lawyers.

You must deal with juror number three. You must do what you do with all problems during a trial, namely, confront them. There are no escapes. Maybe, you start slowly: "If I have said anything during this trial not to your liking, I know that you jurors, sworn to be fair, will not hold that against my client." Or: "It may be that you prefer my adversary to me, but I trust that will not affect your decision in this case." Are you beginning to melt that monument of prejudice? Maybe. You're not sure.

Then go on to the others. Forget her. Don't let her impair your argument to the others. Be an optimist: if during deliberations she represents the enemy's view with blind prejudice, she may cause the remaining jurors to coalesce in your favor.

Now you turn to all the other jurors, but they all turn away with equal disdain. It's universal. They all hate you. You cannot now resign from the bar. What do you do? You keep going with your full might. You spare nothing. You make your summation the most logical, the most persuasive, the most compelling argument ever heard in the old courthouse.

You eyeball them. You reach out eye to eye. You do not flinch. Your cause is just. You prove to the jury that nothing but prejudice and irrelevancies stand between your client and a favorable verdict. You smile. You cry. You cajole. You advocate. The ship might be sinking and the crew overboard, but let no man dare say, ever say, that you struck the colors.

"How To"

The neophyte is not satisfied. The young lawyer wants specific examples of "how to" be courageous. "Show me a courageous summation." "Tell me how to be courageous," is the ultimate demand of the beginner. The reply is trite but true: every case is different. No one can tell you. Courage wears many faces. Courage merely means doing our duty honorably, irrespective of the consequence.

Is there a secret to it? Maybe! A little philosophy helps. Once you realize that defeat is not the end of the world, does not mean disbarment, disenfranchisement, banishment, loss of family, property and liberty, you will be more willing to try your case, take the consequences, and enjoy your life.

Should we include a course on "Courage" in law school? No. It might be considered pretentious, and anyway "Character" is harder to teach than "Evidence." More likely we will continue to keep it a secret and be surprised as the daily combat of trial reveals the inner natures of a new generation of trial lawyers. Sometimes the bombastic will lack courage and the modest will possess courage as quietly as an oak.

In a society increasingly automated, mechanized, and impersonal, the constant challenge to the character of the lonely advocate offers a rare and exhilarating opportunity.

THE TEN MOST COMMON TRANSGRESSIONS AGAINST THE MANNERS AND MORALS OF ADVOCATES

FRANCIS GOODE HAS LONG BEEN FASCINATED BY THE VENOMOUS trial tactics of Evel Sinic. Trying cases against Evel is like fighting rattlesnakes except Evel gives less warning. Francis has spent a lifetime cataloging Evel's transgressions. He has even discovered a few antidotes.

1. ***The Tricky Brief.*** Evel Sinic likes to win them early. "Go for the Judge's mind" is his motto. His favorite part of a brief is the "Facts." Judges may know the law but lawyers "know" the facts.

Evel begins: "This type plane has never before crashed." He knows of three previous crashes but thinks no one else does. Sinic loves the inadmissible. "The decedent was once arrested for disorderly conduct." He knows what's admissible. He just likes to taint the Judge's mind.

Evel never cites unfavorable authority. He asks, "Why cite a case if it doesn't help you?" He cannot stand those lily-livered lawyers who are candid with the Court.

How does he get away with it? He never exchanges briefs with his opponents. Amusingly, however, he always accuses his opponents of slipping things to the judge. "They didn't give me that, Your Honor," he protests, and he protesteth too much. He

believes the rest of the world is like him. He sees knavery everywhere because he sees his own reflection.

ANTIDOTE: Get his brief. How? Be suspicious. When dealing
with the likes of Evel Sinic, say, when first meeting the trial judge,
"I assume all briefs will be exchanged?" Most judges will impa-
tiently reply, "Of course." Then innocently ask: "Will we exchange
when we submit to the Court?" Judge: "Of course." Fine. You have
made the point. Sinic likes to give you his brief two days after he
gives it to the judge. He's all heart.

If you learn Sinic has sneaked a submission to the Court,
expose him. You might start with a smile, "Evel, you sly one,
you're not up to your old backdoor ways, are you?" If he does it
again, put it on the record. Most appellate judges know Sinic
already.

When you get his brief, read it with a microscope. Look for
the inadmissible. Seek out the falsehoods. Make Evel rue the day
he pulled that on you. Read his cases. Sniff out those that have
been reversed. Give the Court the case he didn't cite. Expose his
shabbiness. The judges don't appreciate Mr. Sinic.

In short: Destroy the little that remains of the credibility of
Evel Sinic.

2. *Injecting the Inadmissible.* Inadmissible evidence is elixir
to Evel Sinic. He thrives on it. He needs a fix at least once a trial.

Knowing remarriage of the widow is inadmissible, he says,
"Mrs. Wedlock—oh, beg your pardon—that's your new name, I
mean Mrs. Bereaved." On cross, he likes to ask upright citizens,
"Have you ever been convicted of a crime?" and takes their denial
with scornful disbelief. When he doesn't like an exhibit in evidence, he casts doubt on it: "That's not on my copy, Judge" says
he while emphatically waving a blank piece of paper. He always
asks for stipulations in front of the jury. Knowing that mention of
"compensation" is improper, he asks his opponent to concede:
"That was decided by the Compensation Board. Don't you agree,
John?" This familiarity is usually accompanied by a honeyed smile

behind which lurks the jackal's sneer. Sinic plants answers to general questions. "What did you then do?" asks he of his client, the defendant. Answer: "I gave our safety manager the lawsuit papers and told him, I think we have no insurance so this claim could bankrupt us and a lot of people might lose their jobs."

Evel Sinic secretly looks upon himself as a creative and forceful advocate. "Who else could be this resourceful?" cackles he to himself.

ANTIDOTE: Get assigned to Judge Veteran. He's kindly but strict and will deal sternly with Evel—probably in front of the jury.

The problem is getting Judge New, who is not yet up to Evel.

What can we do if assigned to Judge New? Object? Yes. But we may not want to further emphasize the damage in front of the jury. Then go for the sidebar. "Your Honor, may we approach the bench?" There protest and place the objection on the record.

Should you ask the Court to admonish the jury to disregard what Mr. Sinic said? Sometimes, yes. But be careful. It may merely reinforce the poisoned darts in the minds of the jury. When Sinic slips in "compensation," you might say "I'm confident the jury will follow your instructions to disregard, Your Honor, but will you also advise them that compensation benefits have to be repaid?" Mr. Sinic usually gets very sullen when that is charged.

If the damage is too disastrous, move for a mistrial. But be careful. You may be winning and that's what Sinic wants. You may have spent much of your client's money on the trial. Use judgment. If there must be a mistrial, ask the Court to assess costs against Sinic. Judges should not hesitate to impose that sanction.

APPLYING THE BRAKES. An ounce of prevention is often better. Use the motion *in limine*. At the beginning of the trial see Judge New. "May we have a direction that no lawyer will mention the remarriage of my client?" This may slow even Evel down.

Every dog is allowed one bite. But after the first transgression, you should go for the mind of Judge New. Persuade the

Judge that if Sinic is "nailed," it might not happen again. Impose, impose nicely, but impose on the Judge. It is the Court's burden to restrain these rambunctious rodeo advocates who know no law but their own success.

One last counterpoison: When Mr. Sinic spills a little arsenic into the trial, you have about one second to retort, based upon your life's entire experience—a retort which will undo the harm, which will not offend the Court and which will not be in bad taste. You say that's extraordinarily difficult? I know—that's why some trial lawyers retire early.

3. *Making Silent Movies.* Evel Sinic loves the story about the lawyer of olden days who put a wire in his cigar so that the jurors would fixate on the ash which, miracle of miracles, never fell. Sinic usually drops books on the floor during his opponent's opening. He thinks it the height of wit to pour water on a table rather than into a glass as he pretends to be completely enraptured by his opponent's summation. He leaves copies of inadmissible but favorable newspaper headlines and photographs on counsel's table in full view of the jurors. He admires the lawyer who brought a package to court, letting the jury speculate whether it was the plaintiff's amputated arm. When representing the defendant in a death case, he has Ms. Fatale, his attractive female assistant, sit in the courtroom alongside the male plaintiff, a widower. She asks him what time it is. He tells her. She thanks him with a pat on his hand. The jurors think the widower is not bereaved anymore.

ANTIDOTE: Expose the viper. Somehow identify the female assistant in front of the jury. "Oh, Mr. Sinic, perhaps your assistant, Ms. Fatale, seated in the back, has the exhibit." One bold lawyer even called Ms. Fatale to the stand to identify her. Evel's bald head turned three shades of crimson.

In jury selection, anticipate Mr. Sinic. "What the Judge tells you to disregard will be disregarded, right?"

As to his other shenanigans, have your own assistant sit in the courtroom. You can't have eyes in the back of your head to see all of Evel's capers.

4. *Speeches Called Objections.* At the heart of Evel's advocacy is the "talking objection." He'd give up every other impropriety if he could keep his speeches which follow the magical phrase, "I object."

"I object, this isn't his first accident, you know." This usually brings plaintiff's counsel to a boil.

"I object. I didn't go to law school in Cambridge like some people I know." This works well with certain urban jurors.

In many ways, Sinic has a genius for obfuscation. He knows how to involve the judge. His opponent is conducting a proper and effective cross-examination. Sinic uncoils and hisses: "Now that's objectionable. He can't use that record. I've covered everything in that record. Judge, will you look at this record and see if I haven't covered that." What is he talking about? Cross should cover what was covered on direct. Evel believes he is smarter than everyone else and that if he keeps on talking he can do or say anything.

He depends on the judge to go fifty-fifty on all rulings. He knows that if half his baseless objections are sustained, he is way ahead. He believes the jury will remain lost in the fog of personalities.

Sinic is brilliant at being the victim. No matter how egregious his conduct, he is always the aggrieved one. To a perfectly proper and damaging question by his opponent, Sinic will howl, "That's outrageous. He's getting close to the area we discussed, Your Honor. Judge, I hate making these objections. I don't enjoy it at all. But what can I do to protect myself? Judge, I ask you to make him stop."

Evel delivers more messages than Western Union. His client is being cross-examined:

Q. *"Did you ever talk to your lawyer, Mr. Sinic?"*
A. *"No."*

"Objection. That's a sly question. It's perfectly obvious my client discussed this case with me many times but only as to the facts of the case, and we don't want to get into the attorney-client area."

ANTIDOTE: I repeat: Get assigned to Judge Veteran. He will put Sinic in jail or at least in his place.

Beware of Judge New, who takes the easy way out. "Now you fellows both know better than that." Then with a sheepish, ingratiating smile to the jury: "You know, the lawyers always get a little carried away." Only one of the "lawyers" was getting carried away and that one should have been put in his place.

Again, it is important to exhort the judge in the absence of the jury. Urge the judge to run a tight ship, to avoid donnybrooks. "Make both of us behave!" Ask the judge to observe who instigates the clashes. Ask the judge to admonish Sinic to desist. This may be easier for an older lawyer, but many a judge will respond to a respectful plea.

If judicial help doesn't arrive, you may again have to fall back on all your inner resources for that instant retort. "I object to counsel's telling the witness the answer he wants." "Mr. Sinic isn't under oath." "I want the witness, not the lawyer, to testify." Jurors aren't fools. Sometimes they will have had enough of Mr. Sinic. He has a way of going too far.

5. *Coaching the Witness.* British barristers do not prepare witnesses. American trial lawyers do. Much preparation is legitimate and proper. Language naturally used by a client may be better replaced with softer substitutes. The word "crash" may become "contact." Truth has not been violated; the change is a mere refinement. The witness has trouble recalling the scene. Let her visit the scene with you. That may even serve truth by enhancing accuracy.

The advocate lives on a thin and perilous edge. It is easy to cross the line. Some preparation is improper and even reprehensible. Mr. Sinic suggests, "Perhaps it was 6 P.M. when the snow stopped, not 2 P.M.?" Or, "The police never gave you a warning about your rights, did they? Did they?" And a felon goes free.

A "lecture" on the law may become a coaching session. Sinic carefully explains the proof necessary to prevail: "It helps in these cases if there was wax on your shoes after you fell. Oh, you say there was." Little manipulations lead to larger ones. "If only someone saw you leaving the store. . . ." "Oh, your friend did see you from her window." Evel Sinic never seems to have trouble finding a witness.

When his clients are being cross-examined, his arms are in constant movement. He gives more signals than a third-base coach.

ANTIDOTE: Be a good cross-examiner. "You were in Mr. Sinic's office eight times before you testified? You never discussed the case? He videotaped you? Was this a dress rehearsal? Have you noticed Mr. Sinic moving his arms?" Plant the seeds of suspicion.

Do not fear rugged cross. Expect it when taking on Sinic. Know there will be at least one surprise witness. Even with no statements or depositions to use on cross, you can be formidable. Nothing is more exhilarating than the "pure" cross of attorney against witness when the attorney knows the witness is lying.

"How long were you at the window?" "Why?" "You saw your friend hurt?" "You never came out?" "You never told the police?" Bite like the Gila monster and never let go.

6. Appealing to the Baseness of Human Nature. Evel thinks other human beings are just like him. He appeals to that which is base and cunning in human nature. He slinks in the shadows. He implies that the old plaintiff is surrounded by her family during trial because they hope to inherit money from the lawsuit.

Sinic is a master of ethnicity. His assistant is always mysteriously of the same racial or ethnic background as most of the jurors. His intonation of names is devilish. "Mr. Gold" or "Mr. Giorno" or "Mr. Grady" or "Mr. Garcia" in Evel's mouth resonates with hidden meaning. He either curries favor with jurors of like background or murmurs deeply to the darkest recesses of their hatred.

Your client has been in a car crash. He asks, "Did you have a bottle of gin with you?" "No?" "Did you tell the police about a bottle of gin?" "No?"

There, of course, is no bottle of gin. You wait all trial for evidence of a gin bottle. It never comes. He was just feeding human suspiciousness. He has done it for years and sometimes gotten away with it. Why? Because jurors aren't perfect. They're all too human. They are willing to believe the worst about other people.

ANTIDOTE: Come out of the shadows. Go into the sunshine. Expose his lies. Confront hatred. Sometimes people can be nice. Look for that which is good in people. Make the jurors believe in something. Maybe you. Maybe your case.

> SUMMATION: "He is an officer of the Court. He has to prove what he claims. He told you there was a gin bottle. There wasn't. Sinic isn't a witness. He broke faith with you. This isn't a game. Do not accept ugly appeals. You are the conscience of the community."

> JURY SELECTION: "My client, Mrs. Douglas, is black. She is entitled to no special favors. But she is entitled to as fair a trial as anyone else. Do you have any bad feelings? Please tell me how you feel. We're strangers. I must depend on you to be honest." Go for it. It's no time to be bashful.

7.   *Intimidation.* "When the facts and the law are against you, attack your opponent." This is a rare lecture given by Sinic to a new associate. (Associates do not stay long in his office.) Evel believes in trial by personality. "If you've got a weak case, distract the jury." Sometimes his opponents unwisely take the bait.

During jury selection, Evel will turn on Mr. Naive and say, "I am sick of your office pulling this stuff." Mr. Naive is flustered, red-faced and speechless. This is the first case his office has had with the incorrigible Sinic. Mr. Naive is barely able to utter the word "unprofessional." During the recess, Evel, a short but physical man, lurks in the corridor waiting until Mr. Naive is alone. He sidles over and whispers so no one can hear "Unprofessional am I? I'll take you downstairs and you can show me just how professional you are." This conversation will be denied. But Mr. Naive is beginning to unravel. He is not accustomed to Pier Seven advocacy.

During the trial, Evel glowers at poor Mr. Naive. Evel refuses to talk to him. Mr. Naive is growing unnerved. Evel has been hinting there is something "unholy" about the case. During a heated exchange, he turns on Naive and shouts "I charge you as being the very author of this scheme." The judge cautions both lawyers to desist.

WHAT SIGNALS?

Later that day, Mr. Naive is quietly sitting in his chair while his client is being cross-examined. Evel isn't doing too well. All of a sudden, he turns on Naive. "Stop it. I saw you giving signals. I'm not stupid, you know." The flabbergasted and sorrowful Mr. Naive barely manages to lamely protest, "I did not signal."

Evel is counting on the jurors to love a street brawl. Life can be dull. Many a juror welcomes a good show to relieve the day's tedium. Needless to say, Evel is guilefully nice to the jurors. The implication is clear: Evel is only cross with Mr. Naive because Naive is a bad man with a bad case. And Mr. Naive is wilting. He is losing his will. Perhaps he will settle the case for less than he thought.

ANTIDOTE: Be brave. The world of trial lawyers is divided between the soft and the strong. Guard against softness. Have the will to try a case against anybody, anywhere, under any circumstances. You may be polite and decent—but that doesn't mean you're weak. Many a bully is a faker and not really that tough. You will stand there even if a tank rolls over you. The street fighters hold no fear for you.

Appeal to the judge and make a record. Most judges won't tolerate this nonsense. Lawyers who engage in this conduct imperil the very verdict they seek.

> JURY SELECTION: Anticipate Mr. Sinic: "Personalities and personal attacks have no place in a lawsuit. You agree? You won't be distracted?"
>
> SUMMATION: "Sinic had no case. He therefore went against me. It may be very entertaining but you're not here for that."

But above all, be controlled. Keep your temper. Evel wants you to be angry. He wants you to take his bait. Once you're on to him, it's easy not to bite. Be a smart fish.

Put a smile on your face. Not only can a soft word turneth away wrath, it can irritate Evel to distraction. Look at him amusedly as if he were a bug. Wit is the sharpest of our weapons and the ultimate achievement of human intelligence. Use it. Turn the tables on him. "He that diggeth a pit shall fall into it."

8.   *Discourtesy, Rudeness and Other Incivilities.* On Evel's wall is a sign, "Courtesy Is Weakness." He summarized his lawyer's creed in his article, "Litigation Is War."

Evel passes notes with a flourish when the other lawyer addresses the jury. He scrapes his chair when his opponent examines a witness. He always stands between his adversary and the witness to block the view.

Evel delights in the last-minute continuance. When representing criminal defendants, he files at least 100 applications before trial, most without any merit, and then protests the unconstitutional denial of a speedy trial.

Evel revels in motion practice on the eve of trial. He bills by the hour. He is terrified of the new procedures under which judges meet early with counsel to eliminate motions. Eighty percent of his practice is the making of motions, most of which could be avoided by a telephone call. Evel wouldn't know how to write an affidavit without being nasty. If he couldn't vent his spleen in those affidavits, he'd have to go for additional therapy. Evel never gives an accident report unless an appellate court orders it. Evel's rule about X-rays is absolute: they are for his eyes only. He explains his failure to comply with court orders with some of the greatest American fiction ever written. His motto is: volunteer nothing. To a request for witnesses and records in his control, he scowls, "Subpoena them." But the genius of Evel is at his greatest when a jury slip is issued. He disappears. At moments like this, not even the FBI could find him. His philosophy is that of the warrior: grind your opponent into the dust.

ANTIDOTE: Be courteous. It's contagious. It will make for a better profession and, irony of ironies, it might even help with the jury. Be calm. Don't let him rile you. "Your Honor, may I wait a moment for Mr. Sinic to get his chair in place?"

Sit back and relax. Sinic will hurt himself more than you ever could. The judge and jury are watching him. Long trials are bad for Sinic: his true nature reveals itself.

9. *Slithering Through the Back Door on First Names.* Evel specializes in judges. He collects them the way some people collect stamps and coins. Sheer ecstasy descends on Evel when he feels safe enough for the first time to call a judge by his or her first name. He has a list of his "first name" judges. There are eighty-three of them presently. He hopes to hit 100 before he dies as a testament to his career at the Bar.

Most of the judges are on to Evel. They smile knowingly at each other as Evel works his way through a meeting of judges going from "Thad" to "Mort" to "Margaret" and finally back to dear old sweet "Billy" who is the "fairest and most brilliant of all jurists" although it has been noted that Evel has cast that superlative on a goodly number of dear, sweet judges that very night.

Evel believes that of the three elements that make up a lawsuit, the facts, the law and the personalities, "personalities" are undoubtedly the most important. Evel plays to the judge. He makes it a practice to arrive early when on trial. He brings coffee and doughnuts. He sits with the clerks telling war stories in the "back" behind the courtroom. Evel strongly believes in doing "public relations" with the clerks. They are part of the "personalities." By being there early, opportunity occasionally knocks. The judge arrives in the robing room. There is a nice country lawyers' atmosphere of friendliness. Evel sees his chance and slithers through the back door to visit with the judge. Evel may put his toe in the water gingerly with a comment about the United Nations and then, if the coast remains clear, offer the judge one of the doughnuts. If all goes well, Evel then goes for it: "John, I'm worried about that model they want to introduce. . . ."

BEWARE OF THE CLERKS

Most judges deal easily with the Sinics of this world. A mere raising of the eyebrow suffices to tell most lawyers when they've gone too far. But occasionally, Evel will find a "Judge John" who succumbs to backdoor advocacy.

And when Evel has a friendly clerk, beware. Amazingly, that clerk is always riding the elevator when the jurors return from lunch. He often says in a loud whisper, "That guy trying the case with Evel would do anything to settle. His case is desperate."

ANTIDOTE: You get there early, too. Be glad to see Evel. Tell him you'll bring the doughnuts tomorrow. Join Evel and "Judge John" in the robing room and share your concerns about the United Nations. Ex parte Evel might even start sleeping later in the morning.

If the problem persists, you might have to make a record. But before you do, stop in to see the judge. "First-naming" judges is an overrated talent; many a jurist doesn't like it. No judge wants to be known as someone who is unfair. Sometimes you have to be bold. Tell the judge, "I don't dare call you 'John.' Does my opponent expect favors?" Good trial lawyers, unlike ostriches, deal with their problems.

Chat with the clerks. Some of them are quite human and on to Evel. They might like to see the "new face" get a fair deal and put Evel in his place. If the clerks persist in favoring Evel, ask for a charge that the jury disregard any comment made by court personnel.

Give the judge and the clerks the presumption of fairness. Don't ride into town with a chip on your shoulder. There's always time to fight.

10. *The Inflammatory Summation.* You haven't lived until you've heard Evel sum up. As a young prosecutor, he always said "I wouldn't bring this case unless I personally believed in the defendant's guilt." As a defense counsel in civil cases, he cries "This case will bankrupt us. We're a poor little corporation." Sometimes he uses the alternate ploy of mock humility: "If this were such a big case, they wouldn't hire me to defend it."

Then one day he got a plaintiff's case and pulled out all the stops: "In all my years at the Bar, I have never seen negligence more criminal than that of the Hartless Company which put profits before little people like Sara Trusting whose husband now lies in his grave because they put dividends before decency. Compare poor Sara Trusting, penniless, with this rich multinational corporation which has money for everything except safety.

"What's the value of Charlie Trusting's life? You wouldn't have any trouble answering that question if you stood at his graveside like I did and heard his children crying, 'I want daddy.'

"I knew Charlie when we were both in the seminary; a better fellow never lived; a better fellow was never killed by cruelty. And their defense was cruel. Who did they put on the stand? That foul excuse of a witness, Minnie Mendacious—a bigger liar never lived. I wish Perry Mason or Clarence Darrow or Abraham Lincoln would have been here. They'd have known what to do. I'm sorry I'm not much as a lawyer, but I did my best. My clients can't pay big fees for the likes of those Wall Street Lawyers who defend the Hartless Company. I wonder how they can sleep at night.

"And if I fought with the judge, please forgive me. I love this judge. We lawyers call him 'the Little Legal Giant of Bedlam.'

"And let me tell you, I love this City. The City of Bedlam is the finest place in the world to practice law.

"I just love being a lawyer. It wasn't easy. When I was a boy, we lived in a railroad flat without central heating. It was cold, as cold as the Hartless Company.

"And then I grew up to represent a guy like Charlie Trusting. I wish you had known him. He was just a poor slob. He'll never go down in history like Julius Caesar or Babe Ruth or Alexander the Great or Humphrey Bogart, but he was my friend and I loved him and that's worth something.

"In my personal opinion, this is the biggest case in the history of our courthouse. And when you're considering the amount to give don't forget my fee, which has to come out of the verdict. As the Immortal Bard said, 'my soul is full of woe that blood should sprinkle to make me grow,' but I've got to live, too.

"This case is about vengeance. Don't let them get away with it. Hurt them. Make them pay. Let them cry a little like we did.

"My voice is breaking. That happened when I was a little boy and I had to deliver papers on early cold mornings.

"What's this case worth? What's a father worth? I'll tell you. My seventeen-year-old daughter would rather have me than $10 million." (Some may wonder why. He really doesn't have a daughter. It's just a routine he uses in summations.)

"As to the size of your verdict, let me leave you with the words of giants: Eisenhower and Ghandi and Kennedy and

Tolstoy all used to say, 'Let there be millions for justice.' And it's cheap for them to get off with ten million. As Casey Stengel said to the umpire, 'Justice ain't no small thing.' I thank you for your verdict, which I know will be a good one. God Bless you, Jurors. God Bless Bedlam. God Bless America."[1]

ANTIDOTE: Object. Object to each impropriety during the summation. Move for a mistrial. Make a record. Sleep tight. This is a free play. The other team was offside. If Evel wins, he loses on motion or appeal. If Evel loses, he loses.

ANTIDOTES REVISITED

Dealing with dirty tricks is never easy. There is no one right way. Judgment helps. Experience helps. Our choices vary case by case. Sometimes a sidebar conference, another time a motion in limine, and always an assignment to an effective judge is helpful. Other times an assistant sitting in the back will detect the latest ruse. We should anticipate in jury selection, castigate in summation and seek relief in the charge. Our tongue may be blessed with the right retort which delights the judge and jury and leaves Evel sputtering. Talk to the judge. Most want to be fair. Make a record, object, protest, take exception, cross-examine. Motions to strike or for instructions to disregard or for mistrials are among our options. Be brave, be courteous, be professional, be calm, be alert, be bold.

Sometimes we will fail, but more often than not, with character, we may be able to push Evel into the very pit he dug for us.

---

[1] See McElhaney, "Dealing with Dirty Tricks," 7 *Litigation* 45 (1981); Underwood, "Adversary Ethics: More Dirty Tricks," 6 American Journal of Trial Advocacy 265 (1982). I found both articles helpful and suggestive sources from which to borrow along with the unforgettable Laughing v. Utica Steam Engine and Boiler Works, 16 A.D.2d 294, 228 N.Y.S.2d 44 (N.Y. App. Div. 1962), a comic encyclopedia of how not to sum up.

A TALE OF TWO LAWYERS

1.   *Evel Sinic.* Evel lives alone in a large house with many rooms. He owns two Rolls-Royces licensed ES1 and ES2. He dines only in the finest gourmet restaurants, has little time for exercise and has grown obese. Evel never attends meetings for charitable, civic or Bar purposes, has few friends in the law, disdains "do-gooders" and is offended by prattle of a "noble profession." He sees the law as a business like any other.

> *"Ethics and trial lawyers don't mix. Trial lawyers have one job: to win." Evel adds, "Ethics is for the weak who have never been in a courtroom and would be eaten alive if they were."*

Dining alone in the privacy of his home, belt unbuckled, shoes unlaced, expansive after a few glasses of the finest wine, he likes to unfold and be himself. "Life isn't earnest; it's a game," says Evel.

Sinking deeply into a chair of the finest leather on an Oriental rug of the finest weave surrounded by paintings of the finest artists and books of the finest binding and video recorders and televisions and stereophonic equipment of the finest make, Evel cannot help but feel smug about the vastness of his acquisitions.

It surprises him that he is vaguely unsatisfied and discontented with his life.

2.   *Francis Goode.* Francis is also a trial lawyer. Judges and colleagues respect him because he is candid. Francis has quietly reduced a fee for many a needy client. He lives in a small house. His five children do not feel neglected; he has always found time for them even when on trial. "Each generation," thinks Francis, "has to learn the same lesson anew: What does it profit us to gain the whole world if we lose our humanity?"

Before going to bed each night Francis jogs up the same long hill. The cold air and white snow refresh him tonight. He feels good and knows he will sleep well.

THE ART OF SURVIVAL—
SIXTEEN SECRETS

"Old foxes want no tutors."
—Thomas Fuller

"Life is a long lesson in humility."
—James M. Barrie

REMEMBER JEREMIAH SAGE? AT AGE EIGHTY-EIGHT, HE STILL tried cases. How did he do it? Many trial lawyers give up by age forty-four, too tired to go on. Why do some survive while others wither away early?

One rainy night many years ago, while sipping Wild Turkey bourbons at Fraunces Tavern in lower Manhattan, Jeremiah, surrounded, as always, by admiring young lawyers, confided his secrets on the art of survival. He shared the following:

1.   *Never Do Anything* Pro Forma. Samuel Sameness is in a rut. In a medical malpractice case, he always calls the defendant-doctor first. In a product liability case, he always calls the same expert. In a deposition of a subscribing witness to a will, he always asks the same questions from the same form book. He does everything *pro forma.* He tries cases by rote. Compare G. Louis Novator. He ponders the order of witnesses in every case. He searches for an expert who will bring true conviction. He lets the circumstances of each case, not a form book, dictate the format of his questions. His creativity refreshes him.

2. *Take the Hard Case (or Do Not Be Afraid of a Little Pain).* Everyone runs from it—the MacBuster case before Judge Grumplin. The Honorable Ben Grumplin, long on moods but short on learning, has put it down for trial next month. Percy Slither, opposing counsel, as pleasant as a cobra, has already declared, "This trial will be warfare." Your firm represents a landlord in County Poor where only tenants are allowed to sit on juries. The file fills four drawers. The law is uncertain. The facts are complicated. Bill was to try the case, but his ulcer is acting up. Mary cannot do it because she has two briefs to get out. Howard would love to try it but feels he might have a conflict because one of the potential witnesses has a second cousin that Howard's wife once met. They are running. Trial lawyers might be able to fool all the people all the time but never themselves.

ANTIDOTE: Run to the case. Take it. Insist on trying it. Work on it harder than you have ever worked in your life. Difficulties will start to dissolve. Make it a mission. Teach Percy Slither a lesson he will never forget. Revel in the legal intricacies. Master the facts. It is just like life. Nothing ever goes away until you face up to it. A festering boil must be lanced. Your colleagues will admire you; the court will respect you, and best of all you will feel good about yourself. Tough cases make good memories. It is a paradox. "What is most difficult to do is sweetest to see done."

3. *Try a Case You Love.* You cannot blame Wanda Weary for living for her pension. She has tried fender-benders for thirty years. Jock Shillingham only defends tobacco companies. The pay is good, but his friends ask him, "How can you do that?" J. Winston Spats has gained great stature and handsome fees trying antitrust cases. At fifty-four, he seems to be having a mid-life crisis asking everyone big questions about the meaning of life.

Diagnosis of their ailment: All are bored just making a living. Treatment: Try a case for love.

EXAMPLES: Defend the members of a congregation whose church or synagogue is threatened. The fee may be small but the gratitude will be big. A little *pro bono* might enrich the spirit and result in your defending an indigent accused of crime. Variety might spice an otherwise dull trial term. Civil rights and environmental lawyers never seem to tire of their labor. The case that stretches us beyond our ordinary niche may be the only one that nourishes our deepest needs and rejuvenates our spirit.

4. *Do Not Take the Case Home.* At least, not every night. Compare three trial lawyers.

A. Bernie Burden carries the heavy weight of each case with him everywhere. He makes life even harder than it is. He does not sleep well when on trial. He looks more tired in the morning than at night. Bernie worries about everything. He brings every problem home to his wife and children. He wins a lot of cases but he says he cannot do it much longer—too exhausting.

B. Clients certainly prefer Bernie to an indifferent soul like Reginald Bored, who brags, "After 5 P.M., I retire as a trial lawyer." Reginald loses many of his cases.

C. Then there is Lively McThinker. Lively worries about her cases, brings home work but somehow finds time when on trial to see a play occasionally, call another client, read a book. She sleeps well. She comes in fresh every morning. How does she manage? She puts it all in perspective and does not take it home every night.

5. *Never Lie or Cheat.* Percy Slither can never be trusted. He will appear before the court unannounced, falsely telling the judge that he advised his absent opponent to be present. He will stipulate on the phone but deny it in court. He does not care how he wins as long as he wins. At forty-eight, shadows darken his face, and wrinkles crowd his eyes, which dart from side to side always seeking advantage.

Francis Goode celebrated his eighty-eighth birthday by trying a case. His word is his bond. If he had a document, fraudulently obtained, that could help him, he would never use it. Francis has an inflexible rule: never lie to a client or for a client.

Peers marvel at his face, a good face—craggy, cranberry cheeks, clean eyes, a smiling, serene look. He exemplifies an old adage: at twenty, you have the face with which you were born; at fifty, you have the face you deserve.

Long after the Percys of this world slither into oblivion, the memory of Francis Goode will still nourish people.

6.   *Beware of Young Lawyers.* Along comes Kurt Callow. They call him The Kid. He has everything to prove. When he enters a courthouse, he has but one question: who is the fastest gun in town? He needs another notch on his record. Beware. Prepare twice as hard for a young opponent. We never get a pass. We always have to prove ourselves. It is good. It keeps us young.

7.   *Do Not Drink Before Five.* Vin Corker has a way with words. He charms jurors. He disarms opponents with a smile. He works hard. Lately, at lunch, he has taken to giving himself a reward. Sometimes a wine. On occasion, a martini. He rationalizes that it relaxes him. In candor, he depends on it more and more for courage. Sometimes it takes two, perhaps three martinis at lunch to find it. In truth, Vin is known as an easy target after lunch. Opponents save their best question, their most devastating exhibit, their most damaging witness for late in the day. Vin has succumbed to the gratification that has weighed down many a great one.

8.   *Do Not Take Yourself Too Seriously.* When trial lawyers start to think of themselves as important, it is time to change jobs. Humility, the trial lawyer's best friend, not only delights jurors, it makes better human beings.

Exercise for middle-aged trial lawyers who have been told they are wonderful: at the next bar association cocktail party, seek out one of meager rank, perhaps a young lawyer who would be flattered by your attention. Give that young lawyer your total attention, eyes fully on that person. Remember it must be a person who can do nothing for you. Supreme Test: do not move your eyes from that young lawyer even when a federal judge, before whom you have a major case, walks past you.

9. *Do Not Read the Advance Sheets Only.* Gregory Grind regularly reads the advance sheets. He can cite, by number, sections of the federal rules of this and that. He spends untold hours scanning legal memos and every word of his opponents' briefs. He laments that he has not read a novel or a poem since school days. He does not have the time. Gregory does not think deeply about the history and the reasons behind the law. Technically but narrowly proficient, he has become a clerk of the law.

Trial lawyers travel in wide precincts. They must predict the unpredictable: what judges and juries will do with these facts, these witnesses, these rules of law. They need to know a lot. They deal in humanity. They must read more than legal rules. They might learn more from Dickens than from the uniform code of whatever. Exercise for young lawyers wanting to be great advocates after the age of seventy-five: read all of Dickens' novels and all of Shakespeare's plays, and then decide which one (only one) Robinson Crusoe should take from his wreck of a ship.

10. *Read the Advance Sheets.* Of course, keep up. Love the tools of your craft. Prescription for a happy old age: work hard at what you love.

11. *Keep Fit.* Peter Pudgely has worked hard to master the craft of litigation. He works long hours, attends seminars, reads the latest periodicals on advocacy and enjoys his profession. Peter at five feet ten inches and 195 pounds carries thirty to forty pounds of unneeded weight like a suitcase with him wherever he goes. Yesterday, he ran for a train in Grand Central; it took him ten minutes to catch his breath. During trial in the afternoon, he often finds himself embarrassingly close to dozing. He cannot work after supper because he tends to fall asleep. Coming to court in the morning, he has no bounce in his step, no joy in his face. Peter is grossly unfit. He cannot possibly compete in the demanding world of trial lawyers.

Compare Thelma Thinlonger, another trial lawyer. She jogs four miles every morning, watches what she eats and feels great. Alertly, she reacts to every movement in the courtroom, even late in the day.

Remedy for Mr. Pudgely: jog, swim or walk yourself into shape. Watch what you eat, even if you have to deprive yourself of an occasional sweet. A pudgy lawyer suggests indulgence, not a lean and hungry advocate ready to do battle.

12. *Have Other Interests.* Do not be boring. Do not talk only about the law. Suggestions: Join a book club. Be a volunteer at the hospital. Chair a committee to aid the needy at Phoenix House. Take a *pro bono* government job. Do something. One may live as greatly in the law as anywhere else.

13. *Talk to Civilians.* Do not be boring. Do not talk only to lawyers. Talk to plumbers, playwrights, hairdressers, even doctors.

14. *Take Vacations.* Tommy Laborare tried one case after another. He never stopped. He usually won. He prepared for trial with a diligence that delighted clients. Tommy rarely rested. His cases always came first—before himself, before his family. Once he cancelled a trip to Rome with his wife in order to accept a new case that had to be tried in two weeks. He always meant to get around to taking his daughter to Dublin, which she asked him to do many times. He always intended to fulfill his dream of seeing Antarctica, the last refuge of unspoiled beauty. Last year, Tommy, fifty-eight years of age, never sick a day in his life, without warning, had a heart attack and died. Wasn't Tommy silly?

15. *Do Not Worry Just About Winning.* Howard Fearfill has not taken a verdict in years. Everybody knows it. Too bad. He tries a good case, well prepared, strong opening, persuasive summation, knows the law. But he cannot take defeat. Problem: vanity. He thinks more about himself than his client. Pride drags him down. Defeat ages him. He thinks the whole world chuckles at his every loss. In truth, most of the time, nobody is even looking.

Listen to Jeremiah: "Do your best. Let justice be done and forget about winning or losing." Secret: the world does not end with our every defeat.

16. *Laugh a Lot.* (Particularly at yourself.)

CONCLUSION:

These precepts helped Jeremiah Sage reach old age at the trial bar. Keep fit, be ethical, take vacations, have many interests, laugh, do not take yourself too seriously, love your work, be creative, face up to hard problems. Not a bad prescription. Come to think of it, it is not a bad way to get through life for anyone—whether you are a trial lawyer or just a normal human being.

HENRY G. MILLER, a Senior Member of the New York law firm Clark, Gagliardi & Miller P.C., has been actively trying cases for over four decades. He is a former Director of the International Academy of Trial Lawyers and the New York State Trial Lawyers Association, a past Regent of the American College of Trial Lawyers and past President of the New York State Bar Association. Mr. Miller was appointed by New York State Governor George Pataki to serve on the Committee to Review Audio-Visual Coverage of Court Proceedings and by Governor Mario Cuomo to Chair the Temporary State Commission on Local Government Ethics. A frequent columnist in the *New York Law Journal,* Mr. Miller authored, and continues to update, *Art of Advocacy: Settlements* published by Matthew Bender.

ALSO FROM *ALM PUBLISHING:*

Full Disclosure: The New Lawyer's Must-Read Career Guide
By Christen Civiletto Carey, Esq.

Game, Set, Match: Winning the Negotiations Game
by Henry S. Kramer

The Essential Guide to the Best (and Worst) Legal Sites on the Web
by Robert J. Ambrogi, Esq.

Biz Dev 3.0: Changing Business As We Know It
by Brad Keywell

Other Publications Available from AMERICAN LAWYER MEDIA:

LAW JOURNAL PRESS Professional Legal Treatises—over 120 titles available

LAW JOURNAL NEWSLETTERS—over 40 titles available

Legal Newspapers and Magazines—over 25 national and regional titles available, including:

The American Lawyer
The National Law Journal
New York Law Journal

Visit us at our websites:
www.lawcatalog.com
and
www.americanlawyermedia.com